AVIATION
IN SOUTH AFRICA

This book is for all my friends in aviation, particularly those who have lost their lives in pursuing what must surely be one of the more worthwhile professions and pastimes: flying.

HERMAN POTGIETER

AVIATION
IN SOUTH AFRICA
Photographs by Herman Potgieter

JANE'S

First published in the United Kingdom in 1986 by
Jane's Publishing Company Ltd
238 City Road London EC1V 2PU

Photographs © Herman Potgieter 1986
Text © the respective authors 1986

First published 1986

Distributed in the Philippines and the USA and its dependencies
by Jane's Publishing Inc
115 Fifth Avenue New York NY 10003

ISBN 0 7106 0423 8

Printing and Binding by CT Products, London, England
BD4988

PHOTOGRAPHER'S ACKNOWLEDGEMENTS

Without the help and interest of the following people, most of the photographs
in this book would not have been possible; to all of them I am extremely
grateful:

Dave Aronowitz of Frank and Hirsch, Nikon agents in South Africa; Eric
Horvitch of Photo Agencies; Captain Meyer Botha and Nick Venter of SAA;
Colonel Bertrand Retief, Colonel André Bekker, Colonel 'Monster' Wilkens,
Commandant Koos Smit, Commandant Polla Kruger, Commandant Johan
Rankin, Major Ray Houghton, Major Rob Sproul, Captain Terry Pyke,
Captain Steel Upton, Captain Peter Viljoen and Lieutenant Marie Berg – all
of the SAAF; Scully Levin and the Winfield Magnum Team; Dennis Spence
of the Smirnoff Team; Peter Hendricks; Len Wilmans; 'Buzz' Bezuidenhout;
John Pocock; Bob Ewing of EAA Chapter 322; Alan Blain of South African
Aeronews; Tom Chalmers of World Airnews; Kuno von Dürckheim and Slade
Healey of Lansav; Dave Vermaak of Air Cape; Deirdre Farquhar of Magnum
Airlines; Robin Reid of National Airways Corporation; Jeremy Labuschagne
of Court Helicopters; Hugh Flynn and Steve Meyer of Safair; Mike Basson of
Bass Aviation; Chris Briers; Fanie van Rensburg and Bernard Schutte of
Aviation 2000; Steve Anderson; Tim James; Bill Kiel; John Williamson; Tony
Corrie; Bill Harrop; Dave Boome; Peter Celliers of Celair; Dave Anderson of
Ciba Geigy; Dennis da Silva and Fido of Beith. In addition there are many
others who gave invaluable assistance in various ways – especially in the
organization and execution of photo sessions. I cannot list them individually
but take this opportunity to thank them all most sincerely.

PUBLISHER'S ACKNOWLEDGEMENTS

We are most grateful to South African Airways for generously supporting this
project. We must also record our sincere appreciation to Louis Vosloo for his
advice and assistance, especially for agreeing to write the captions to most of
the photographs.

Previous pages: An unusual combination. The Winfield Magnum team's
three aerobatic Pitts Specials fly, near Nelspruit, in tight formation together
with two Harvards of the Central Flying School, SAAF.

Overleaf: Flying in the Drakensberg demands expert airmanship. This
MBB/Kawasaki BK117 helicopter flown by 'Monster' Wilkens and Slade
Healey, has just landed on Champagne Castle in gusty weather conditions.

CONTENTS

INTRODUCTION

BY JOHN POCOCK

This book tells the story of aviation in South Africa. It is not an historical work – though it does of course cover aspects of the past that are relevant to the present. Nor does it attempt to look into the future. It is, in essence, a book of outstanding photographs that comprehensively and splendidly illustrate the multi-faceted world of flying in this country today.

Scarcely any of modern man's inventions have had such a profound impact on his society as the aeroplane. Born in this century, younger than many people still living, the science (and art) of flying has progressed to the point where a London businessman can breakfast at home, wing his way to a three-hour conference in New York and still be back in time for dinner.

This kind of rapid and efficient transport has brought our physical horizons immeasurably closer, and has radically changed the nature of human capability and endeavour in both peace and war. Especially in peace: business activity, sport, agriculture, weather research, geology, geophysics – the list of beneficiaries is almost endless.

The broad spectrum of aviation in South Africa does not differ fundamentally from that in other developed countries. But it does have its special emphasis, its own personality. Ours is a large land, distances between major centres are great, some areas are not easily accessible, and air travel probably features more prominently in our daily lives – certainly in our professional lives – than it does in the lives of Englishmen, Frenchmen or Italians. If you're a farmer buying cattle in the north-western Transvaal, a mining engineer solving technical problems in Hotazel, a geologist investigating ore bodies around Noordoewer, a tourist game-viewing at Moumi, or simply a Johannesburger planning to visit relatives in Cape Town, you'll probably need the use of an aircraft of one kind or another.

However, although the operation of aircraft and their support infrastructure – overhaul and service, airports and airfields – have reached a high degree of sophistication, the civil aircraft manufacturing industry is virtually non-existent. Here economies of scale have dictated progress: South Africa's viably productive population is comparatively small; the demand for local products simply wouldn't justify the capital investment involved unless there was large export potential. The country certainly has the expertise to build aeroplanes; it just doesn't have enough customers. The Atlas Aircraft Corporation, for instance, which was born of necessity, is more than capable of meeting most military

demands, but were it to enter the civilian market it would simply not be able to compete economically.

The local manufacture of microlights, on the other hand, is poised to take off – literally. Because of their extreme simplicity, most of the components needed for microlights can be produced in existing facilities at relatively low cost. Engines and instrumentation still have to be imported but, even with the current unfavourable exchange rates, production of the machines here is still cost-effective. Indeed, the very weakness of the rand could well bring an export-orientated stimulus to the industry.

The rising cost of imports and services in South Africa is seriously inhibiting the ownership and use of private light aircraft, and this, too, will lend impetus to microlighting and other forms of sport aviation. Those in whom the desire to take to the air is strong – and there are many of us – are looking elsewhere in the mid-1980s: not only to the marvellous world of microlights but also to hang gliding and gliding, to ballooning and skydiving.

All aspects of sport aviation are controlled by the Aero Club of South Africa, which is affiliated to the F.A.I. (the Federale Aeronautique Internationale). The Club has nine sections, ranging from aero-modelling to power-flying, and a membership of 5 000.

We live in changing times, and precisely what the future has in store is anyone's guess. There is, however, one abiding certainty: aviation in general will continue to develop with exciting swiftness. New technology is being introduced almost by the month; the makers of passenger aircraft are competing fiercely to carry more people on less fuel; designs are becoming so advanced that those who fly the craft are more in the nature of computer specialists than pilots in the traditional mould.

The search for fuel efficiency in particular (which could, ironically, prompt a return to propeller-driven aircraft) is extending into all branches of aviation. Beech, for example, have developed a new turbo-prop business model in canard configuration that promises to be hugely successful.

Aviation is here to stay: we need it, and our scientific ingenuity will continue to refine it to unimaginable limits. For South Africa, the years to come are not so easily charted; but if, in Sir Winston Churchill's phrase, we should enter a 'calmer and kindlier age', then our industry's technical pre-eminence in Africa will enable us to play a truly significant role in the expansion of aviation throughout the continent.

1

THE FLYING SPRINGBOK
South African Airways

BY DAVE MULLANY

South African Airways, the state-owned national carrier, celebrated its 50th anniversary on 1 February 1984. From the outset the growth of SAA has been linked closely to the progress of South African aviation as a whole, and the pioneering spirit and ingenuity that characterized the early days of aviation in this country was also crucial to the later development of the Republic's national airline.

South Africa is isolated from the mainstream of the West both by distance and also by hostile neighbours to the north. At the same time it is highly advanced technologically. This sophistication, coupled with a determination to overcome all odds, has led to the development of routes and the acquisition and adaptation of aircraft tailored specifically to the country's unique circumstances. The result is a national airline on a par with the world's best.

SAA boasts an impressive number of aviation records. In 1953, for example, it became the first airline outside the United Kingdom to put the world's earliest jetliner – the graceful but ill-fated de Havilland Comet 1 – into regular service. A total of eight Comets were leased from BOAC and flown by SAA crews on the London-Johannesburg route.

In 1956 the airline achieved another record when one of its Douglas DC-7Bs flew from Johannesburg to London in 21 hours, stopping once. This seems protracted by today's standards, but not when compared with the UK to South Africa time of 11 days in the early 1930s.

A year later SAA notched up another world first when one of its DC-7Bs flew from Johannesburg to London, via Cairo, in 17 hours and 45 minutes. This was impressive enough at the time, but the records really began to topple in the 1960s, when SAA acquired the first of the Boeings that today comprise more than 80 per cent of its fleet.

South Africa's first Boeing was the B707-344 intercontinental jetliner, powered by four Pratt & Whitney JT4A turbojet engines and capable of carrying 117 passengers in its SAA configuration. Later variants – the B707-344 B and C types – were equipped with the slightly more powerful Pratt & Whitney JT3D-7W turbofans. SAA became the first airline to fly B707s fitted with full-span leading edge flaps, a high-lift device necessitated by the hot and high conditions at Jan Smuts Airport.

In 1963 came the incident that taxed SAA's ingenuity to the limits and changed the whole face of its international flying operation. The storm had been brewing for months and finally broke on 22 August 1963, when Egypt, Algeria, Sudan and Libya banned all overflying by South African-registered aircraft. In a matter of hours, most of North Africa had become a no-go zone for the South African airline. Fortunately, SAA planners had foreseen such a possibility and contingency plans had already been made for the company's aircraft to fly round the bulge of Africa to Europe, via Luanda in Angola (then still under Portuguese control), and Las Palmas in the Canary Islands. The route switch – implemented at a moment's notice – went without major mishap and not a single flight had to be cancelled.

The airline maintained its Las Palmas route until the early 1970s; it then switched operations to the former Portuguese colony of Ilha do Sal, one of the Cape Verde Islands some 400 km off the coast of Senegal. Today, Ilha do Sal boasts a major international airport with an annual turn-around of one million passengers – some 90 per cent of them on scheduled SAA flights, the rest accommodated on Soviet, Cuban and Angolan airlines.

The wide-bodied Boeing 747s in the SAA fleet also use Ilha do Sal as a one-stop refuelling point for the airline's North American routes. SAA now flies to New York four times a week and to Houston once a week. Before the advent of the long-range B747 fleet, SAA flew B707s to New York via Rio de Janeiro.

South Africa's first jumbo jet was the Boeing 747-244 Super B, a 349-seat aircraft with a maximum take-off weight of 365 100 kg. It was powered by four Pratt & Whitney JT9D-7Q high-bypass, water-injected turbofans with a thrust of 235 kN. A total of seven Super Bs were ordered by SAA, and the first of these – ZS-SAN, *Lebombo* – was delivered on 6 November 1971.

SAA re-wrote the record books again in 1976 with the delivery of the first of six unique, short-bodied B747SP-44 jumbos (the SP designation stands for Special Performance). They were developed by Boeing partly in response to SAA's need for an aircraft that would be fuel-efficient and capable of flying non-stop to the United States or non-stop to Europe around the bulge of Africa. The result was a compact, wide-bodied jumbo 14,6 m shorter than its 70,51 m sisters, with a lower take-off weight (315 246 kg against 365 100 kg for the Super B), better fuel consumption (9 500 kg/hour against 11 200 kg/hour), and an 11 per cent improvement in range (9 260 km against 8 335 km for the new B747-300). SAA's B747SPs carry a reduced passenger load of 282 and are powered by four Pratt & Whitney JT9D-7FN turbofans which develop 222 kN of thrust.

The first B747SP (ZS-SPA, *Matroosberg*) was delivered on 24 March 1976 after setting a new world record for the longest non-stop flight by a commercial aircraft. It covered the 16 510 km from Seattle to Cape Town in 17 hours and 22 minutes.

The JT9D-7Q engines developed for the B747 Super Bs were also built to SAA's particular requirements. Says Pratt & Whitney's senior vice-president Robert Rosati: 'This was the first really high-altitude, long-range engine and it was developed specially to meet SAA's need to fly around the bulge of Africa. It is basically a South African engine. Its reliability is excellent and it is doing good work for us throughout the world today.'

In similar vein, Boeing spokesman Bill Kane reveals that SAA requirements have had a significant bearing on the design of his company's more recent aircraft.

For example: Jan Smuts, SAA's headquarters and the country's principal airport, is in a high-temperature, high-altitude zone (1 750 m above sea level). Both these factors place severe restrictions on range and payload and one of SAA's major requirements is for aircraft that can operate safely and efficiently in such an environment.

In addition, SAA makes relatively few short-haul domestic flights because of the great distances between major centres in South Africa. Consequently, the airline requires planes that are exceptionally fuel-efficient – for reasons of safety as well as economy. Long range and fuel-efficiency are also vital to SAA's international operations: on average, its foreign routes are the longest in the world.

Says Kane: 'The people at SAA have had no small influence on the way our aeroplanes

1

2

4

3

7

8

5

6

1 Well-known South African 'crazy pilot' Scully Levin displays exceptional flying skill in bringing his 1946-model Piper J-3C Cub down on a 'land-based aircraft carrier'.

2 Scully Levin in action again, masquerading as the aged 'Colonel Bunkle' flying for the first time since the First World War.

3 A Westland Wasp HAS Mk. 1, Alouette II, Alouette III and Puma, with a Super Frelon trailing, are flown by candidates on the SAAF's Test Pilot Course.

4 In perfect symmetry, Chris Rademan and Jeff Birch, two of the three-man Winfield Magnum team, give an impressive mirror-flying demonstration in their Pitts Specials.

5 Journalist Jani Allen nonchalantly applies lipstick while Tony Gall rolls his Pitts Special

6 Tim James flies his Cosmos Trike past the Procolor hot air balloon.

7 Peter Viljoen rolls the Aerospatiale Trinidad.

8 A Piper Pawnee Brave demonstrates skittle whacking at an airshow at Virginia Airport.

13

have developed. We've had to build in features that would allow them to take off on a hot day at high altitudes. We've also worked closely with Pratt & Whitney to develop engines which are higher-thrusted for a short period to improve payload out of hot, high airfields.'

SAA presently maintains a fleet of 38 jet aircraft on its local and international routes. The last of the airline's propeller-driven craft – three Hawker Siddeley HS 748s – were sold to Canada's Austin Airways in December 1983. Flagship of the present fleet is the magnificent Boeing 747-344B SUD (Stretched Upper Deck), a modified jumbo delivered in 1983 and characterized by its enlarged, upper deck (17,8 m long) and SAA-configured seating for 394 passengers.

On the domestic front, SAA maintains a fleet of 24 medium-range aircraft, including the only non-Boeing plane in its inventory – the 1972-vintage Airbus Industrie A300, better known as the Airbus. SAA uses seven A300s in three variants – four B2s, two B4s and one C4 – on its prime internal routes between Johannesburg, Durban and Cape Town.

The remainder of SAA's domestic fleet consists of 17 of the successful Boeing 737 short-to-medium-haul jet transport, noted for its exceptional fuel economy. The airline acquired its first example of the type (ZS-SBL, *Pongola*) in 1968, and the twin-engined, 117-seater 'baby' jets have since logged hundreds of thousands of kilometres on the nation's domestic and regional routes.

There are two B737 variants in the SAA fleet: the basic B737-244, and the more recent B737-244(ADV), which has a better payload, increased range and the more powerful and efficient Pratt & Whitney JT8D-17A engines, which afford a four per cent fuel saving over the B type's JT8D-9s.

Between 1965 and 1982, SAA also flew six of the rear-mounted, tri-engined Boeing 727-44s and three B727-44Cs. This aircraft was commercial aviation's answer to the VW Beetle, with a record 1 825 sold up to 1982. Eventually, however, the B727s were sold off in the interests of economy. The B727, in fact, was not particularly fuel efficient and when it was replaced by B737s on all domestic routes, SAA officials calculated the switch would lead to fuel savings of R12,5 million in the first year alone.

Although SAA today operates only jet aircraft, in the past 50 years it has flown some of the most famous piston-engined aircraft ever built. The first planes to be taken into SAA service were acquired in 1934 when the South African government gained control of the ailing Union Airways and renamed it South African Airways.

Among these first aircraft were two of the five DH60G Gypsy Moths brought to South Africa by Major Allister Miller, a British-born Royal Flying Corps veteran who had settled in this country after the First World War.

He had founded Union Airways in 1929 with backing from the Atlantic Refining Company of Africa, and – using two-seater Gypsy Moths – operated a regular mail service between Johannesburg, Bloemfontein, Durban, East London, Port Elizabeth and Cape Town on an £8 000-a-year South African government contract.

Unfortunately the venture did not last: five years after it was founded, Major Miller's fledgling airline was on the verge of bankruptcy. Stricken by a series of accidents (which claimed the lives of four crew and eight passengers and resulted in the loss of a Puss Moth, a six-seater Fokker Super Universal and a Junkers W.34) and a general shortage of money (it was the time of the Great Depression), Union Airways finally collapsed. It was taken over by the South African government on 1 February 1934. South African Airways had been born . . .

When the government took over Union Airways Major Miller's fleet consisted of two de Havilland Gypsy Moths, a de Havilland DH 80A Puss Moth, four Junkers F.13s (with enclosed cabin space for four passengers) and one six-seater Junkers W.34. The total passenger-carrying capacity of the new airline was all of 27 people. This was, however, increased with the acquisition, before the war, of a number of Junkers Ju52/3m's and Ju86s, and four Airspeed AS.6J Envoys. These, together with 29 Lockheed L18-08 Lodestars delivered in 1940/41, were commandeered for use by the SAAF during the war.

Immediately after the war, SAA moved into the growing international market with the inauguration of its famous Springbok Service between Johannesburg's Palmietfontein Airport and Hurn Airport near Bournemouth in England. The aircraft chosen to fly this route was the 12-seater, Rolls-Royce Merlin-powered Avro York, which was partly derived from the RAF's famous Lancaster bomber. SAA's first York – ZS-ATP, *Springbok* – was leased from BOAC as part of a pool partnership venture and the service was introduced on 10 November 1945.

The Springbok Service proved an immediate success and the airline found that even with three flights a week, its fleet of nine leased Yorks was insufficient to cope with the demand for bookings. Consequently, the operation was bolstered in 1946 by the purchase of the first of seven Douglas DC-4 Skymasters and the introduction of a Skymaster service between Johannesburg and London. SAA's 30-seater DC-4s also worked the domestic routes, remaining in the regional service until 1966.

It was also in 1946 that SAA – in an attempt to upgrade and expand its domestic service – took delivery of the aircraft it would eventually operate for longer (24 years) than any other type: the DC-3 Dakota, probably the most famous and certainly the best-loved airliner in history. SAA acquired eight

of these marvellous flying machines and used them on all domestic routes and on its trans-border services until 1970.

The immediate post-war years represented a period of rapid growth and expansion for SAA as the airline extended its fleet and set about developing its local and international networks. In 1947, eight 24-seat Vickers Viking 1Bs were added to the domestic and regional inventory of Lodestars, Dakotas and de Havilland Doves, while in 1950 overseas horizons were broadened with the purchase of four Lockheed L-749A Constellations, which had seating for 50 passengers and – for the first time – pressurized cabins for high-altitude flight. By 1956 the Constellations had replaced all DC-4s on SAA's international routes, and had reduced the Johannesburg-London flying time to 28 hours. In 1956 the fleet of Constellations was augmented by Douglas DC-7Bs – at that stage the world's fastest piston-engined airliners. Another major propeller-driven aircraft to serve with SAA was the Vickers Viscount 813. Seven of these large-windowed turboprops were obtained in 1958 (with an eighth Viscount 818 acquired from Cuba in 1962) and used on SAA's main domestic and regional routes until 1971, when they were sold to British Midland Airways, which uses them to this day.

By the end of the post-war decade, SAA had opened its first London office (1947), created a 76-hour airfreight service between England and South Africa, and had also begun weekly DC-4 flights between Cairo and Johannesburg (1949). One year later, a regular service between South Africa and Israel was created by extending the same route.

During this period the airline also acquired a new international airport – a huge site on the farm Witkoppies, some 12 km east of Johannesburg. On 3 March 1947 the Highveld Airport officially became Jan Smuts Airport, named in honour of the Prime Minister and wartime commander, Field Marshal Jan Smuts. The naming ceremony was performed by one of Smuts's wartime comrades – Viscount Montgomery of Alamein. Jan Smuts Airport was officially opened on 3 October 1953. Three other major airports – Cape Town's D.F. Malan, Port Elizabeth's H.F. Verwoerd and Durban's Louis Botha – were opened within two years.

However, Jan Smuts remains the nation's principal air terminal: a massive commercial aviation facility with a total ground area of 1 330 hectares, a 4 411 m runway, 129 500 m² of terminal buildings, and the largest hangar in the southern hemisphere (opened on 25 November 1982, after a five-year project costing R36 million). The airport also features eight restaurants, nine bars and sufficient parking space for 5 000 vehicles. More than four million passengers (of whom 2,5 million are domestic and 1,5 million are international travellers) use the terminal each year, while annual freight movement amounts to some 110 million kg.

Jan Smuts serves a total of 27 airlines, including the national carrier, and has a staff of 540. On 1 August 1984 the inauguration of a 3 500 m runway doubled the airport's capacity from 40 to 80 flights an hour.

SAA has come a long way in half a century. The airline started out in 1934 with a complement of eight aircraft and a capacity of 27 passengers. Today it operates a fleet of 38 sophisticated jet aircraft with a total passenger capacity of 7 250. From a cargo of five mailbags and a contract worth 8 000 pounds a year in 1934, SAA has grown to the point where it now carries more than 7 760 tons of mail and 70 000 tons of cargo each year, with annual airfreight earnings amounting to some R130 million.

When SAA introduced the country's first regular, fare-paying passenger flights, no-one gave a thought to the notion of in-flight service provided by a team of trained attendants: this refinement was introduced only in 1946. Today, however, SAA fields a team of 1 500 cabin crew who will serve anything up to 8 000 meals a day. In the course of their duties, cabin attendants on a single international flight may each walk a total of 16 kilometres.

At the beginning of the 1960s, SAA had 28 aircraft, 2 750 employees, and an operating revenue of just over R19 million. Today the airline employs 11 500 people (2 250 in the technical division alone) and generates income of more than R1 000 million a year.

Back in 1934, SAA flew only between Johannesburg, Durban, Port Elizabeth and Cape Town. By 1984 the airline was flying to 44 major destinations on all five continents. In 1934 the airline offered four flights a week: now it operates 325 a week (253 domestic, 40 regional, 32 international) over a route network extending 195 995 kilometres across the globe (23 503 km domestic, 9 605 km regional and 162 887 km international).

Fuel consumption figures provide yet another startling contrast between the old and the new. On the Springbok Service in the mid-1940s, a 12-passenger Avro York took 32 hours and 30 minutes and consumed the equivalent of R9 038 worth of fuel in flying from Johannesburg to Bournemouth. Today, however, an SAA B747 SUD with 376 passengers on board can fly from Jan Smuts to London's Heathrow Airport in just 12 hours – but at a vastly increased fuel cost of R67 485.

SAA confounded its critics (and no doubt a great many of the advocates of deregulation too) by showing a profit for the 1983-84 financial year. This amounted to only a few million, but even so it was a remarkable accomplishment for a government-run airline – especially in view of the depressed state of the aviation industry worldwide. SAA had budgeted R1,5 billion for the period in question, but spent only R1,2 billion. The ensuing profit was the airline's first in four years.

SAA officials offer the following reasons for the turn-around: rationalization of fuel and personnel costs (which together comprise about 50 per cent of the total SAA budget); streamlining of timetables and flight operations (on some routes, for example, smaller aircraft are substituted if a scheduled Airbus is not fully booked); fuel-saving benefits of the super-efficient B737 fleet since the withdrawal of the airline's B727s at the end of 1982; and – probably the most important factor of all – the 1983 world oil glut that enabled SAA to bargain for better prices from the major fuel companies.

The question of handing over the national airline to private enterprise has been discussed at official level. In 1982 the state-appointed Margo Commission of Inquiry into Civil Aviation debated the pros and cons of deregulation in general terms, even suggesting an easing of SAA's domestic stranglehold by permitting South Africa's smaller carriers to operate freely on certain regional routes – particularly those sectors that had proved uneconomical for SAA. However, the Commission refused to be drawn on the matter of total deregulation, and made no formal recommendation.

Although the government has accepted more than 80 per cent of the Commission's 300 recommendations concerning the industry, few of these have been implemented because of 'a lack of funds'. In South Africa, perhaps more than anywhere else in the West, commercial aviation remains a Cinderella industry in the eyes of state authority.

As for the future of SAA, airline officials predict further expansion of its international sectors, particularly in the East (SAA serves Hong Kong and Taiwan, but not Japan); development and increased flexibility on its regional and internal routes; long overdue improvement of its domestic terminal facilities; and an upgrading of its freight-handling equipment to cope with an anticipated increase in volume in the remainder of the decade.

And, according to a newspaper interview given by SAA's Chief Executive in January 1986, the airline's fleet of Boeing 737s is to be replaced, in the late 1980s, with more fuel-efficient Airbus 320s.

2

THE WIDENING WEB
Regional and feeder airlines

BY JOHAN LABUSCHAGNE

Beyond South African Airways and the service it provides to the ten major centres within the country is a multitude of 'other operators' – mostly small, privately-owned aviation companies with limited resources and few opportunities for expansion. Air transport is regulated very strictly at the upper end, allowing no competition with the national carrier. Towards the lower end are courageous entrepreneurs who provide a service which has become indispensable.

South Africa is acknowledged as one of the world's most beautiful countries, its tourist attractions providing a wealth of interest to some 600 000 visitors every year. It is also a highly industrialized country with a dynamic business community and one of the most successful economies in Africa. All of this demands an effective transport infrastructure, and it is here that the feeder airlines make an important contribution.

Of course, the feeder airlines have to compete with road and rail transport. Although passenger rail traffic is diminishing, the road

1 Precision flying at its best: one small mistake could spell disaster for Manfred Strössenreuther as he flies inverted at almost zero altitude at La Mercy Airfield, near Durban, in a Czech-designed Zlin 50L.

2 A formation of three diverse aircraft, but all with Pratt & Whitney Wasp radial engines. Both the Harvard and the three-engined Ju52/3m (CASA 352L) are powered by nine-cylinder 550 hp R-1340 Wasps, while the Beech Model 17 Staggerwing has a less powerful nine-cylinder 450 hp R-985 Wasp Junior.

traveller clearly still appreciates the convenience and independence provided by his own car. However, the fuel crisis of the mid-1970s and the accompanying restrictions persuaded many motorists to become air travellers.

Operators face a number of difficulties. Initiating such a business is expensive – particularly now that exchange rates and interest rates have greatly increased the price of capital equipment. Spares, routine maintenance and fuel are also very costly.

On the positive side, South Africa has a system of good airfields equipped with fair navigational aids, and the weather is mostly ideal for flying.

Although some private aviation companies were registered during the mid-1930s, the true feeder airlines evolved from charter operations during the early 1960s. Initially, the National Transport Commission guarded the interests of the national carrier and only awarded traffic rights for scheduled operations on condition that SAA could take over the routes at any time. As a result, there was no real incentive in the long term. SAA recently undertook to provide direct services between the ten main centres only, and other operators have been granted the right to fly the routes between these centres provided that they land in-between and do not undercut SAA tariffs.

When SAA rationalized its fleet – retaining only jet aircraft – new possibilities were provided for the established regional airlines of Air Botswana, Royal Swazi Airlines and Air Lesotho. More recently, Bophuthatswana acquired Mmabatho Air and Transkei established Transkei Airways. The aircraft used by these operators range from single-engined four-seaters to two-engined turbine aircraft and four-engined jets with intercontinental capability. The technology is equally varied.

Second in size only to SAA, Safmarine's aviation interests (Safair Freighters, Namibair and Air Cape) represent a substantial investment in this country's air transport network. Beyond that, Comair and Magnum Airlines are at present the most significant.

SAFAIR FREIGHTERS

This company has a large and sophisticated operations network spanning several continents. Its aircraft, including the huge Hercules cargo carriers, fly anywhere – from Europe and the Unites States to the tropical jungles of Africa. The pilots happily take on the challenge of ill-prepared runways, sometimes even landing on dry river beds. With its 16 aircraft, Safair has become the world's largest commercial operator of the Lockheed Hercules aircraft.

Its operations have taken it further north than any other South African carrier: Safair planes flew to the Canadian arctic wastes of Melville Island, where a landing was made at East Drake – an airfield built on floating ice barely two metres thick and floating above 100 m of icy sea, approximately 20 km from the nearest land. To the south, Safair pilots have flown to Rio Gallegos at the southernmost tip of Argentina.

The idea of a South African air cargo company was conceived by the late Dr G. S. Kushke in 1969, when he was chairman of the board of Safmarine. He reasoned that the rapid growth of the air cargo industry, worldwide, indicated a future trend towards this form of transport.

Safair's first aircraft, a Lockheed L100-20 (registered ZS-GSK in honour of Dr Kushke), arrived in September 1970 and was christened *Boland*. There was great excitement in the beginning, but then the terms of the operating licence were tested and found to be prohibitively restrictive. Eighteen months later the operation seemed doomed. But the company was saved at the last moment when it was granted its first transport contract.

From then on its growth was rapid, and by the end of 1976 the company had taken delivery of its full fleet of longer-fuselaged L100-30s. The growth in traffic did not keep pace, however, and for a long time Safair lingered in the doldrums. Today, though, Safair is a dynamic and highly successful entity with diverse operations and interests throughout the world. Its recent acquisition of two Boeing 707-344Cs is ample proof of this. Its 'go anywhere, anytime' service provides equally well for the delicate translocation of endangered wild animals and the transportation of rugged earthmoving and construction equipment.

AIR CAPE

Clifford Harris, whose construction empire was well established by the early 1960s, decided that an aircraft was needed to provide transport to his various construction sites. It was later found that the aircraft was under-utilized, so Harris obtained a charter licence and formed Air Cape on 10 August 1962.

The expansion in charter work was rapid, and by the late 1960s the company had ventured into scheduled services, operating a DC-3 along the east coast on behalf of SAA. Air Cape then established its own scheduled routes – with limited success. At the time the company operated DC-3, Beechcraft 99A and various light, twin-engined aircraft.

Today Air Cape is wholly owned by Safmarine, and all its scheduled flights are undertaken by its HS 748 and Swearingen Merlin IVA aircraft. Their routes take passengers over some of the most scenic parts of the country – from Cape Town via Oudtshoorn, George and Plettenberg Bay to Port Elizabeth, and from Cape Town to Walvis Bay via Alexander Bay and Lüderitz.

NAMIBAIR

Namibia is a vast country, in which travellers once had no choice but to drive very long distances over devastatingly poor roads. The first attempt to provide an air passenger service was the establishment of South West Air Transport in 1935, an undertaking that had only limited success.

After the Second World War, people returned to the territory with renewed enthusiasm – and a great deal of valuable aviation experience. The economic doldrums of the 1930s were forgotten, the future beckoned, and in November 1946 South West Air Transport was again registered.

Suidwes Lugdiens was formed at the same time, but the company could not obtain any operating rights. In 1947 the two companies were amalgamated under the name Suidwes Lugdiens, whose first scheduled services (using Navions) were launched between Windhoek and Grootfontein via Otjiwarongo, Outjo and Tsumeb. Twelve years later, Oryx Aviation (formed in 1956) was also merged with Suidwes Lugdiens.

The West Coast fishing industry began to boom during the early 1960s, and an air link became essential between Cape Town and the coastal towns of Lüderitz and Walvis Bay. As a result, Namibair was formed. The airline was based in Walvis Bay and operated only chartered services. In 1966 Namibair took over Suidwes Lugdiens and amalgamated its combined operations under the name of Suidwes Lugdiens. Safmarine later acquired a controlling interest in the company, which is presently owned by the government of the territory and Safmarine. In 1979 the company was again re-named, once more becoming Namibair.

The airline operates into the forbidden 'Sperrgebiet', and along the Skeleton Coast, and its pilots have included men of character and great experience, men like Heinz Schubert and 'Spookie' Zeip, who flew for the Luftwaffe during the Second World War.

Namibair presently provides services (using light, twin-engined aircraft) from Windhoek to Tsumeb, Rundu, Katima Mulilo and Grootfontein as well as from Windhoek to Ondangua via Tsumeb.

In addition it offers a daily service from Windhoek to Swakopmund and Walvis Bay and (in conjunction with Air Cape) flights from Walvis Bay to Alexander Bay via Lüderitz. It also carries mine labourers in Convair CV580 aircraft.

The future of Namibair depends largely on the territory's political and economic destiny. It is possible that services will extend to Keetmanshoop and Upington, developing to the stage where bilateral agreements could be reached with South African Airways to provide services to destinations in South Africa. Other regional and international services are also possible.

COMAIR

Comair was conceived in a dusty tent in Egypt in September 1942 when two SAAF pilots, A. C. Joubert and J. M. S. Martin, were idly dreaming of what they might like to do after the war. It was about two weeks before the battle of El Alamein.

The dream soon turned into a substantial reality: Commercial Air Services (Comair) was registered in 1943 and two years later the company secured the Cessna dealership. The founders also discovered a number of war surplus single-engined Fairchild UC-78 aircraft in Cairo, ten of which they bought for £1 000 each and ferried to Rand Airport between March and May 1946. None of the pilots had civilian flying licences or passports; neither did the aircraft have certificates of airworthiness or registration. But SAAF uniforms and RAF markings on the aircraft took care of these problems, and apart from rough-running engines over the swamps of the southern Sudan – caused by water in the fuel – the trip was uneventful. These aircraft were used for charter work, satisfying an increasing demand by business people for air travel during the period just after the war. The service was later extended to Nairobi, Cairo, Leopoldville, Luanda, Stanleyville, Accra and Lagos.

The first scheduled service was inaugurated in July 1948 with the introduction of a new four-seater, single-engined Cessna 195 flying the return route from Rand Airport to Durban via Kroonstad, Odendaalsrust, Bloemfontein, Bethlehem and Ladysmith. This daily service was very reliable but unfortunately not very profitable. By May 1949 it had been reduced to a daily return flight between Rand Airport and Welkom. It is interesting to note that when Comair was about to drop its Welkom flights, the Anglo American Corporation stepped in to subsidize the service, which afforded the corporation an important link with the developing Free State goldfields.

Two de Havilland Rapides were bought from Central African Airways in October 1949 and introduced on the Welkom route. Each could accommodate eight passengers, and although travellers did not like their slowness, the Rapides were reliable and relatively cheap to operate – so much so that in one month the service actually showed a profit of 13 shillings and 6 pence! The airline later acquired two de Havilland Doves, which were put into service in May 1951. The public responded favourably to them but they were unreliable and costly to operate: break-even point was four full fares beyond their maximum seating capacity.

Taking the attitude that any change would be an improvement, the company next acquired two Lockheed Lodestars from East African Airways in Nairobi. With the purchase of these aircraft – they entered service in April 1953 – there at last came signs of a turn-around. The Welkom service was extended to Durban during the late 1950s, and by 1960 the company was operating well into the black.

Passenger loads grew beyond the Lodestar's capacity of 17 seats, and extra backup was provided when Douglas DC-3 Dakotas were put into service in 1963. In the same year, Comair began a daily service to Phalaborwa using a Cessna 205. Growth was so rapid that within five months Lodestars were also flying on this route.

Today, Comair operates three 44-seat Fokker F27-200 Friendships and two Douglas DC-3 Dakotas on its scheduled services. With these aircraft they provide a high standard of service from Jan Smuts Airport to Phalaborwa, Skukuza, Richards Bay, Pietermaritzburg and Margate. The route to Richards Bay is operated on behalf of SAA, while Magnum Airlines operates the Welkom route on behalf of Comair. The airline also has a safari business, which links up with its flights to Skukuza.

MAGNUM AIRLINES

The founders of Magnum Airlines believed that the way to success was not to start off with a modest route and build it to the stage where it became profitable, but instead to purchase and consolidate established operations. Consequently, in 1978 they acquired Air Lowveld, Avna Airlines and Emric Air. They took over the Natal division of National Airlines the following year, and in 1982 they bought a 50 per cent stake in United Air's scheduled operations. Magnum has since sold its interest in United Air, but has retained the scheduled routes.

With the appearance of the Kerzner 'kingdom' at Sun City, Magnum launched a shuttle service between Grand Central Airport and the Pilanesberg, using Britten-Norman Trislanders and offering up to 30 return flights a day on the route.

Magnum believes in the high-frequency, low-density approach, which offers their passengers a greater choice of flights. With this in mind they operate a number of Piper Chieftains and Swearingen Metroliners.

The future of Magnum certainly appears secure, a fact that is substantiated by the two de Havilland Dash 8s it has on order. This will be the first time that any privately-owned South African airline has put new aircraft of that size into operation.

CITI AIR

This, the newest name in feeder airlines, was known as Margate Air before August 1985 and was originally conceived as a means of attracting vacation traffic while providing a convenient facility for Margate businessmen.

With its handsome fleet of light single- and twin-engined aircraft (consisting of Piper Cherokee 6s, a Piper Chieftain, two Cessna 402s and one Cessna 310) Citi Air serves Pietermaritzburg, Ladysmith, Newcastle and Vryheid from Durban. It also connects Durban with Margate and provides a regional service to the Transkeian capital of Umtata.

EASTERN AIRLINES

The Coastal route between Durban and Richards Bay was pioneered by Emric Air, later taken over by Magnum Airlines. Eventually the route was acquired by SAA and operated on their behalf by Comair. Recently, however, the route was awarded to Eastern Airlines, which services it in collaboration with Citi Air.

GIYANI AIRWAYS

Giyani Airways, formerly Letaba-Lugdiens, was established in 1974 as a result of the fuel crisis and the road speed restrictions that followed. It was initially owned by a Tzaneen businessman but has since become the property of the Gazankulu government.

The airline started out with a Beechcraft 18 twin-engined aircraft; today it owns a Cessna 412 Golden Eagle, two Cessna Titan 414s and one 17-seater Swearingen Merlin IVA. With these it provides services between Jan Smuts Airport and Giyani, as well as flights to Pietersburg and Tzaneen.

Although the prospect of any route expansion seems remote, the airline does hope to use larger-capacity aircraft in the future.

THERON AIRWAYS

The growth of the Northern Transvaal was responsible for the airline's inauguration in 1976. Its passengers are mostly businessmen who travel between Jan Smuts Airport and Ellisras, Alldays, Messina and Louis Trichardt in two light, twin-engined aircraft.

BORDER AIR

Based in East London, Border Air provides a daily scheduled service to Umtata (using either a Cessna 402 or a Beechcraft Baron). Its flights also link East London with various coastal resorts along Transkei's Wild Coast. Future expansion of the airline depends on the development of Transkei and the Eastern Cape.

NATIONAL AIRLINES

Wings Airways was born during the late 1970s with the development of mining activities in Namaqualand and the Northern Cape. Although National Airlines had existed long before that time, it was only in November 1982 – after the takeover of Wings Airways – that the joint operation was recognized as a fully-fledged feeder airline.

National Airlines uses Beechcraft 200 King Airs to connect Lanseria Airport near Johannesburg with the small centres of Kuruman, Aggeneys, Alexander Bay, Lime Acres and Postmasburg.

NAMAKWALAND-LUGDIENS

The railway line from Cape Town to Namaqualand terminates at Bitterfontein, and the area north of that point was once served only by road transport and, later, by chartered light aircraft. The first scheduled service to the area, offered by Namakwaland-Lugdiens, was from Youngsfield or D. F. Malan Airport in Cape Town to Springbok. The airline now operates three Piper Navajos, two Piper Chieftains and one Piper Aztec. On 1 February 1986 Namakwaland-Lugdiens joined forces with National Airlines to provide an enlarged service to the north-western Cape.

3

BUSINESS ON THE WING
Corporate and commercial flying

BY JOHN POCOCK

Whether or not to buy a business aircraft – that controversial and very expensive tool – is an issue which more than a few top executives find unsettling. It is apt to raise the blood pressure of shareholders and has caused less experienced aircraft salesmen to seek new employment.

Business aircraft are clearly not for everyone. There are many large companies that – for economic or logistical reasons – could never justify ownership of an aircraft. However, the number of companies making use of business aircraft (either through ownership or charter) has been steadily increasing over the years, and the reasons are readily apparent: the primary function of business aviation is to increase productivity, so for the executive whose hours are worth hundreds of rands the business aircraft is a real boon. It offers two critical benefits – flexibility and time-saving.

There are other benefits too: the cost of a business aircraft as well as its running expenses are tax deductible when the aircraft is used for business purposes or the procurement of revenue. Such an aircraft also enables executives to avoid the delays, lost luggage, queuing at check-in counters, over-booked flights, standing in the rain waiting for buses, X-ray machines and the many other irritations associated with scheduled air travel. An executive en route to an important business meeting hardly needs this kind of stress. In addition, most places with airfields are not served by scheduled flights; business aviation offers excellent security; and many business aircraft feature a 'boardroom'-type layout, which provides a working environment that allows the executive to use his time profitably.

There is no single, dramatic event to which one can point and say: 'That was the start of business aviation in South Africa.' Instead, it evolved as the need arose and as the aviation entrepreneurs saw and developed opportunities. To fully appreciate the present state of business aviation in this country it is necessary to take a look at the background of some of the companies involved.

In order to have aviation there must be aircraft, so the story obviously starts with the manufacturers. All the top manufacturers of business aircraft are represented in South Africa, their representation ranging from individuals operating from offices with hardly more than a secretary and a telephone, to fully established companies with all the necessary infrastructure to supply and support the product they offer.

In 1939 Piet van der Woude obtained the Piper agency for southern Africa. But the war stopped development, and Piet became aerodrome inspector for the duration, flying around the country in a Hornet Moth. A story is told about his getting lost on a flight in the Cape and ending up over the sea, out of sight of land – and out of fuel as well. Not fancying his chances as a long-distance swimmer, and not knowing in which direction to swim anyway, Piet was lucky enough to find a ship next to which he could ditch his plane. When he was taken on board, the ship's captain – who thought Piet might have been carrying a message for him – told him in no uncertain terms that had he known that the pilot was merely lost he would never have picked him up (he was concerned because stopping the ship was dangerous with U-boats around).

After the war, Van der Woude ordered about 100 J-3 Cubs and wrote to O. B. Oberholzer, who was in Italy at the time, asking him to join the company as chief engineer. Oberholzer duly joined the Pretoria Light Aircraft Company (PLACO) on 13 December 1945 – and he is still there to this day, in spite of several changes of ownership.

One of the biggest names in corporate aviation worldwide – and certainly in South Africa – is Beechcraft. This agency was originally held by Wally Stern's Aviation Corporation. In 1967 it passed to National Airways Corporation, an organization launched as a charter company. NAC had held agencies such as Aero Commander and Mooney, but relinquished these dealerships when it took on Beechcraft.

NAC is regarded by observers as an innovative and aggressive organization. Certainly it has established itself as the best Beechcraft dealer outside the United States. The present managing director, Graeme Conlyn, is also president of the Commercial Aviation Association and is very much involved in business aviation in South Africa.

The story of Comair, which secured the Cessna dealership in 1945 – an association that has lasted to this day – was related in Chapter 2.

The Aero Commander has also been reasonably successful in South Africa. Its manufacturer has been owned by Rockwell and

Gulfstream, and has been represented by several South African companies – the latest of which is Astra Aircraft Corporation, which has made its mark in the larger-aircraft market as the South African agent for Lockheed.

It can thus be seen that a large choice of aircraft is available to the business community and to individual owners. These range from the single-engined owner-flown luxury machines (such as the pressurized Piper Malibu, Beechcraft Bonanza and Cessna 210) to the super-luxury executive jets and turboprops (such as the Cessna Citation, Gates Learjet – sold in South Africa by NAC – Beechcraft King Air and Piper Cheyenne). Most companies operating the latter group of aircraft employ highly trained, professional crews.

A section of the market also catered for by the big manufacturers is the 'weekend' pilot. He is usually a member of a flying club and most of his aviation activities are recreational, though he might do some business flying as well. The smaller Cessna 150s, Beech Musketeers and Piper Tomahawks are thus a familiar sight at most of the country's airfields. There are many flying clubs in South Africa, some of which – for example the Durban Wings Club, the Cape Aero Club and the Johannesburg Light Plane Club – go back almost as far as aviation itself in South Africa. Unfortunately the high cost of flying has reduced this market considerably.

At 31st January 1986, South Africa's civil aircraft population was as follows:

Piston-engined	3 447
Turboprops	101
Jets	57
Helicopters	167
Gliders	270
Balloons	36
	4 078

These figures include the fleets of both SAA and Safair. Graeme Conlyn estimates that about 2 000 of these aircraft are used for business purposes.

The mining and associated industries have long been one of the biggest users of business aircraft. Mineral deposits are frequently located in remote areas – Orapa, Jwaneng and Selibe Pikwe in Botswana, Finch mine, Sishen, Hotazel and Aggeneys in the Northern Cape, and Rossing, Oranjemund and Rosh Pinah in Namibia are but a few of these.

All such mines have to be visited by management and engineering staff, to say nothing of the people who provide the various essential services. Companies such as Anglo American and Gencor have entire fleets of business aircraft, all aspects of whose operation, scheduling, maintenance, flight training and associated administration are handled by flight departments – and their standards are so high that their safety records would make many airlines envious. Anglo American has aircraft based at many of its mines, and these machines also provide an emergency service

in the event of accident or injury. The Corporation uses helicopters for shorter-range executive transport.

Anglo Alpha Cement operates two Gulfstream Commanders, which provide links with its factories at Dudfield and Ulco. Escom also uses Commanders, as its operations are spread very widely.

A number of companies own executive jets with intercontinental capabilities. For example, the Rembrandt group has a Falcon 50 and Anglo American a Gulfstream III. The use of these aircraft on overseas trips provides the managements with security and a great deal of flexibility.

A smaller executive jet, the Cessna Citation, is very popular worldwide: there are some 15 of these aircraft in South Africa – owned by companies such as Grinaker, Premier Milling, Anglo American, Brian Stocks and Kangra Holdings. Many businessmen fly their own aircraft, for purposes that range from carrying day-old chicks to flying freight at night.

The Margo Commission of Inquiry into Civil Aviation completed its findings in 1982: one of its conclusions was that a large and modern fleet of civil aircraft is important to the country, both from a strategic and an economic point of view. What do some of the men at the top think?

Cor Beek, executive director of the Commercial Aviation Association: 'The attitudes to business aviation are changing. This is due to a number of factors, among which are the findings of the Margo Commission and the efforts of the CAA. Business aviation is not yet fully developed in South Africa as many people here do not yet fully appreciate the meaning of time.'

Dave Novick, managing director of Comair: 'During the 1970s we experienced a boom in civil aviation. This was due to the good business climate existing within South Africa and the very good rand-dollar exchange rate prevailing at that time. Unfortunately, the reverse is true today – a bad economy and a weak rand have resulted in many aircraft being exported. Few new business aircraft will be sold in the near future, and companies will tend to make their existing aircraft last longer, or purchase good second-hand machines. If, however, our relationship with Black Africa improves, we can expect a great increase in aviation activity, as our infrastructure can be of great help to those to the north of us'.

Graeme Conlyn, managing director of NAC and president of the CAA: 'The Government is beginning to make sensible use of general aviation. This indicates a recognition of the industry, and we are beginning to see the effects of this with such developments as the recent decrease in the price of aviation fuel. Deregulation in the industry is beginning to appear more of a reality.

'Full implementation of the recommendations made by the Margo Commission is es-

sential for the healthy growth of commercial aviation in this region. The depressed period we are going through now is a passing phase, and in spite of it NAC has not experienced any major drop in revenues. Beechcraft are embarking on new projects, and their Starship should be seen in South Africa at the end of 1987. This new-technology, high-speed, high-altitude, fuel-efficient turboprop uses the canard principle, and will make quite an impact on business aviation.'

Business aviation plays many rôles. One encounters King Airs, Citations and other aircraft from South Africa at the most surprising places north of our borders. Business contacts are being established all over, and observers have expressed the hope that these will help to pave the way to a better future.

SPECIALIZED AIRCRAFT

Commercial aircraft are used for many purposes other than transport, most of these activities falling into the category known as 'aerial work'.

The Aircraft Operating Company, which was involved in aerial photography for the purposes of mapping before the war (using Puss Moths and a BA Double Eagle), was taken over by the SAAF at the outbreak of hostilities. After the war the company went back into aerial mapping and geophysical surveys. Its present fleet consists of a Bell 204 helicopter, a Beechcraft Baron, a Cessna 404 and two Dakotas.

Crop spraying now plays a very important rôle in the agricultural industry, but some of the earliest spraying done in South Africa was in fact to eradicate tsetse fly in Northern Natal. PLACO was involved in this programme, flying Piper Cruisers modified by O. B. Oberholzer, who pioneered the spray equipment used. He turned the fuel tank on the aircraft's right wing into a spray tank, removed the starter motor and fitted a spray pump in its place. Later, fuselage tanks were installed.

Avex Air, headed by Mike van Ginkel and Nick Turvey, is currently engaged in a tsetse fly eradication programme in the Okavango Delta. All flying is done at night because the temperature inversions help the spray to settle.

The company uses Piper Aztecs, which are fitted with ultra-low-volume equipment to enable an aircraft carrying 500 litres of insecticide to fly for three-and-a-half hours, covering an enormous area. Litton navigation systems are used – without which night-time navigation would be impossible.

A number of crop spraying companies operate in South Africa, and it is quite common for them to team up with chemical companies. For example, Boland Lugspuitdiens of Malmesbury once operated a partnership with Agricura, who subsequently acquired its own crop-sprayers and is today one of the biggest spraying companies in the industry.

Its work ranges from normal agricultural spraying of insecticides, fungicides, weed-killers and fertilizers, to the eradication of Quelea finches and red locusts (using a Bell 206B helicopter).

The older Piper Super Cubs, Pawnees and Cessna Agwagons have to a large extent given way to the much larger Piper Pawnee Braves, Thrush Commanders and Grumman Agcats and Kingcats. Some of these aircraft are turbine powered and can carry up to 2 200 litres of liquid – allowing 70 hectares to be sprayed with one load.

Orsmond Aerial Sprayers in Bethlehem, one of the largest crop spraying companies in South Africa, has a fire-fighting contract with SAPPI and is also involved in weather modification. Fire-fighting is conducted by 'water bombers', which are modified Turbo Thrush Commanders that can drop almost 2 300 litres of water on a fire in about one-and-a-half seconds. A spotter aircraft detects fires and within a very short time the 'bombers' are on their way. A number of landing strips are located throughout the forests, each equipped with water-loading installations. This method of fire control has already saved millions of rands, and the contract has been running for five years.

Weather modification and hail suppression – techniques that have proved very successful in Israel and the American state of Kansas – are handled mainly by the Department of Transport and the Department of Water Affairs. Organizations that have also been associated with hail suppression are Sentra-Oes and Laeveld-Tabakkorporasie. The idea behind their programme was the reduction of insurance claims resulting from hail damage. Potential hail storms were seeded with silver iodide, which had the effect of turning hail into rain. Unfortunately the project was uneconomical and also met with much resistance from farmers – for all sorts of highly colourful reasons.

Weather research is presently being undertaken in Nelspruit by C.I.C., using a Lear Jet, and in Bethlehem by Orsmond Aerial Sprayers, using a Turbo Commander 690. The aircraft fly through the clouds, sampling temperature, pressure, vertical velocity, droplet size and ice particle size. If a decision is made to seed the cloud, silver iodide (or dry ice) is released. The resulting precipitation is monitored by another aircraft. The whole operation is controlled from a highly sophisticated ground radar base. There is a great deal more to learn, however, and the programme is to a large extent still in the research stage.

HELICOPTERS

'When you need a helicopter, nothing else will do.' This statement, made by a helicopter manufacturer in its advertising brochure, is very true. Helicopters can go virtually anywhere, their scope being limited only by human imagination. South Africa's helicopter industry grew – quite logically – in areas where fixed-wing aircraft were unsuitable. Once these early helicopters were operating, it was not long before companies – ever watchful for new opportunities – began developing the industry into less obvious areas. Since the local helicopter industry is relatively young, most of its pioneers are still with us – and their personal stories recall the kinds of adventure that most people only dream about.

There are basically three non-military groups of helicopter operators in South Africa: the dealers or sales outlets, the commercial operators and the private owners (made up of companies or corporations, government departments and private individuals).

Among the first to operate commercially in South Africa was United Helicopters (a subsidiary of the giant Bristow Helicopters of the UK), which was responsible for the SABC-contracted survey for the FM network. United used Hiller UH-12E helicopters crewed by Bristow pilots brought here for the purpose.

In the early 1960s two companies appeared that were to have quite an impact on the South African helicopter scene. One was Helicopter Services, started by Dan Pienaar and two partners, and the other was Autair. Among the projects undertaken by the latter in those early days was a survey of the Durban-Johannesburg pipeline, and game conservation work for the Kruger National Park. Some of the game-catching techniques developed then are still used today, and game work continues to form a significant part of the operations of helicopter companies in this country. In 1966 Autair was awarded a contract by Marine Diamonds to provide a service to the diamond barges off the Namibian coast, transporting crews and supplies between the shore and the barges (using Sikorsky S55 helicopters).

On 11 February 1968 an event occurred that was to result in a world first for the South African helicopter industry and open a new and lucrative field for helicopter operations. A French tanker, the *Sivella*, ran aground off Green Point while being replenished by a launch. The ship was not damaged and was refloated next day, but the incident prompted newspaper shipping writer George Young to remark upon the dangers of oil tankers being serviced so close to the coast. Young's article in the *Cape Times* was seen by Ted Huddlestone, a senior pilot with Autair, who sent it to Ted Spreadbury, the head of Autair in southern Africa.

The wheels began turning, and on 12 June 1968 a Sikorsky S55A (ZS-HCL) with Ted Huddlestone as captain and Ted Spreadbury and Ivan Grove as crew, conducted a trial service to the *Dorcasia*. On 6 September in the same year the world's first commercial ship service by helicopter was launched when an S55A (ZS-HCM) flew to the tanker *Mobil Libya*. The closure of the Suez Canal further ensured the success of the undertaking.

Autair was later bought by Court Line International, a fixed-wing operator from Gatwick. When this company went into liquidation in about 1974, Court Line Helicopters was taken over by Murray & Roberts and the Van Zyl family, becoming Court Helicopters. By this time the company had been involved in a wide variety of undertakings, including game catching, crop spraying and survey work.

Court was noted not only for its flight operations. In 1978, when a Sikorsky S61L crashed on the roof of the Pan Am Building in New York, Court tendered successfully for the damaged helicopter. The New York City authority did not want the machine to be airlifted off the building, so a team of Court engineers – directed by Martin Gericke – dismantled most of the aircraft and brought the sections down the lift shaft of the building. The machine was brought to Cape Town, where it was re-built in the Court workshops. At the same time it was converted to the S61N configuration and given the designation S61NC. Registered ZS-HHP, it was the only S61L to have undergone this conversion. When Court was later awarded the contract to supply the *General Mosconi* (an Argentinian rig), the helicopter was sent out to Argentina.

Developing along slightly different lines, Helicopter Services had in the meantime moved to Baragwanath, where they were operating a Bell 47-G4A on a powerline inspection contract for Escom. Bristow Helicopters then bought 60 per cent of the company and brought in some Hiller UH-12E4s. These were sent to Mozambique, where Helicopter Services had formed a company called Hepal (with John Vinagre) to undertake an oil survey. Helicopter Services were also agents for Sud Aviation and became the first company to operate a turbine helicopter commercially in South Africa when they introduced an Alouette II into their fleet. In the early 1970s Bristow bought the remaining 40 per cent of Helicopter Services, and one of the company pilots, Vin van Buuren (an ex-SAAF helicopter pilot), became manager. The company was later acquired by Court.

Towards the end of 1973 a number of events occurred that led to the birth of what is probably South Africa's best known helicopter – the Radio Highveld helicopter. John Pearce, Johannesburg's traffic chief, became interested in helicopter traffic control. Mike Lindridge of Astra Aircraft, the Bell helicopter dealers, had been talking to the SABC on similar lines, and Vin van Buuren became involved in the discussions. Shortly afterwards, Van Buuren left Helicopter Services and joined up with John Nash, Astra's chairman, to launch what was to become Republic Helicopters. Their first contract was for the Radio Highveld helicopter service, for which they used a Bell 206B Jet Ranger (ZS-HDU). 'Ollie' Olivier provided the commentary.

With Vin van Buuren's expertise and Nash's backing, Republic Helicopters grew fast. By 1978 Soekor had been operating offshore for about ten years, their oil rigs being serviced by Court. In 1979 Republic took over this contract, launching its service to Sedco 708 at Hondeklip Bay. Republic also pioneered the first helicopter ambulance service in Africa, and as a result of this and other contributions to the helicopter industry Vin van Buuren was named 'aviation man of the year' in 1983. He remained with Republic until their takeover by Court, when he joined NAC to start NAC Helicopters.

While all this was happening, a pilot named Peter Piggott – who had flown for both Helicopter Services and Autair – was starting an operations and sales company called Heliquip. This company initiated the first helicopter management contract in South Africa, operating a Gazelle for Iscor. That contract is still running, Iscor presently owning an AS 350B Ecureuil (Squirrel) bought from Heliquip, which is now the Aerospatiale dealer and part of the PLACO group.

Most civilian helicopters are military derivatives, and for many years were special-purpose machines. But with the advent of the Bell 206B Jet Ranger, business began to take an interest in the helicopter as a commuter aircraft. The first Jet Ranger sold in South Africa went to Brickor. It was flown by Peter Pinell, who had previously piloted Alouette IIs in the Lesotho mountains for Jack Scott, the mining magnate. During the 1970s Paul Nash – John Nash's son and known to most South Africans as a champion athlete and former holder of the world 100 m record – also proved his worth as a helicopter salesman, moving a large number of Jet Rangers into South Africa. Many of these machines were handled by Republic Helicopters on management contracts and some were also used for charter work, thereby earning revenue for their owners.

Up until the early 1980s, sales activity was brisk. Comair sold many Hughes 269s and some Hughes 500s: some of the former were used in the game industry, where their manoeuvrability was important, whereas the speed and good handling characteristics of the 500s found wide appeal. Aerospatiale came up with the Squirrel, which has also proved very popular, and Astra began selling Robinsons R22s, which feature low cost and reliability.

Twin-engined helicopters have not, as yet, made a significant mark on the corporate scene: so far, only SATS and Henlook have operated them. Possible reasons for this are the costs involved (the weak rand has made aircraft very expensive) and the fact that most single-engined executive helicopters are very safe. In 1981, though, Herpa Motors of Krugersdorp (which owned a Jet Ranger) obtained the agency for Messerschmitt-Bölkow-Blohm (MBB) of Germany. This company's BO 105 and the larger BK 117 are remarkable

helicopters. They are twin-engined craft equipped with a rotor head that allows them to perform the sort of manoeuvres that most helicopter pilots avoid. There are 14 of these machines in southern Africa, and the owners include the governments of Lesotho, Ciskei and Venda.

What do some of the men who are closely associated with aviation in South Africa feel about the current state of the country's helicopter industry and its future prospects?

Cor Beek, the executive director of the Commercial Aviation Association: 'There is no point in having a helicopter if it has to land at an airport. Facilities are what we need.'

Vin van Buuren of NAC: 'The major growth is likely to be around the oil industry

and community services, but innovation will play a big part.'

Peter Piggott of Heliquip: 'Helicopter schedules in New York are, to a large extent, subsidized by the airlines, so why not here?'

Although the current recession is retarding the growth of the helicopter industry, the future is promising.

The development of the promising Mossel Bay gasfields and the Lesotho Highlands Water Scheme, in particular, will create enormous potential for helicopter operations. When this is coupled to an increasing use of helicopters in daily life (for rescue services, traffic patrol, news gathering and tourism), the prospects for the industry look very good indeed.

4

CASTLE IN THE SKY
The South African Air Force

BY LOUIS VOSLOO

The South African Air Force is probably unique among the air forces of the West. Forced by political circumstances to operate a largely outmoded inventory of aircraft types, it is nevertheless manned by pilots and crew regarded as among the world's best. The reason for this is simple: like the Israeli Air Force, the SAAF is small, but its rôle has resulted in the development of a combat-seasoned corps of professionals whose operational flying experience puts them on a par with the best in the world's major air forces.

The SAAF is not the largest air force in Africa (this distinction goes to Egypt), but it may safely be said to be the most effective. This is not surprising, since it has a proud history spanning more than 60 years. In addition, the SAAF was involved in both the Sec-

ond World War and the Korean War, and in recent times has seen extensive combat experience in the operational areas of northern Namibia and southern Angola.

As far as the age of its aircraft goes, the SAAF has to make do with a motley collection of types whose ages span some 40 years. In fact, several of the types – for example the Dakotas, the Harvards and even the early Canberras – are older than the pilots who fly them. Even the most modern combat type, the Mirage F-1, has seen more than a decade of operational service with the SAAF, and appears likely to continue in its rôle for some time to come.

Recently withdrawn aircraft such as the Sabre and Shackleton are not being replaced because a United Nations Security Council resolution passed in 1977 made it mandatory for all UN member states to observe a strict arms embargo against South Africa. As far back as the early 1960s, the Security Council passed a resolution calling for a voluntary arms embargo against this country. The United States implemented this resolution immediately, and the seven Lockheed C-130B Hercules transport aircraft delivered in 1963 became the last US type to be sold to the SAAF for more than a decade.

Britain followed suit soon afterwards when the Labour government abruptly cancelled an option the SAAF held for further Buccaneer aircraft. The closest Britain has subsequently come to selling combat aircraft to South Africa was in the early 1970s, when it met a follow-up order for six additional Westland Wasp anti-submarine warfare helicopters to replace Wasps lost since delivery of the original consignment a decade earlier. In another deal with the UK, South Africa acquired seven Hawker-Siddeley HS-125 Mercurius VIP jets. These aircraft were the last British types to be procured. In 1984 it was reported that unsuccessful attempts were made (the matter was even raised during talks between British Prime Minister Margaret Thatcher and the then Premier P. W. Botha) to evaluate British Aerospace BAe 748 Coastguarders as replacements for the Shackletons.

The United States, however, has supplied the SAAF with aircraft in recent times – albeit in small numbers – though they are all conspicuously non-combat in nature, being light VIP aircraft. The first of these was a batch of seven Swearingen (Fairchild) Merlin IVAs, delivered during 1975 and 1976. When they were found to be unsuitable (after eight years' service) they were replaced by three other light aircraft from the USA, among them two Beechcraft 200C King Airs which joined the SAAF's VIP squadron in September 1983.

Combat aircraft were supplied by France and Italy – neither country heeding the voluntary arms embargo against South Africa. This allowed the SAAF to procure no fewer than 106 Mirages from France during the period 1963-1977. Italy, in turn, permitted South Africa to build its Aermacchi MB326 jet trainer under licence – an agreement that led to the establishment of South Africa's own aircraft industry in the form of the Atlas Aircraft Corporation.

Since the UN Security Council resolution of 4 November 1977, no new 'front-line' aircraft have been obtained and this, allied with the completion of the Impala Mk. 2 production, means there is no prospect of large-scale re-equipment for some time to come. Overcoming this problem is the main task of the Atlas Aircraft Corporation: the maintenance and updating of the country's front-line aircraft must be continued.

For the time being, however, the SAAF Mirages can more than adequately hold their own, an assertion that was graphically illustrated on 6 November 1981 and 5 October 1982 when No. 3 Squadron's Mirage F-1CZs shot down Cuban-piloted MiG 21s over Angola after they had posed a threat to South African forces. A further, well-remembered incident occurred on 8 July 1981, when a lone MiG 17 flown by a defecting Mozambique Air Force pilot penetrated South African air space and was quickly intercepted by two Mirage F-1AZs of No. 1 Squadron.

The SAAF's association with the Mirage family of fighters dates back to 1963, when the famous No. 2 'Cheetah' Squadron became one of the first units outside France to re-equip with the Mirage IIIC. These venerable delta-winged interceptors, now based at the ultra-modern air base at Hoedspruit in the Eastern Transvaal, are still an important component in South Africa's air defence system.

Right through the 1960s and early 1970s the number of Mirage IIIs delivered to the SAAF grew progressively as sub-variants of the aircraft were acquired, each fulfilling a special rôle. After the Mirage IIICZs (as the South African version of the IIIC was designated) came a large batch of Mirage IIIEZs with more complex, multi-mission radar and a longer range. While still regarded as a front-line aircraft, the Mirage IIIEZ (alongside the two-seat Mirage IIIDZ and IIID2Z trainers) equips No. 85 Combat Flying School, fulfilling the vital rôle of training SAAF pilots in the use of sophisticated weaponry in combat situations. Apart from a small number of two-seat Mirage IIIBZ conversion trainers, No. 2 Squadron also has a tactical reconnaisance flight of Mirage IIIRZ and IIIR2Z aircraft equipped with an array of cameras in the nose instead of radar.

The SAAF's pride – and its knock-out punch – is its force Mirage F-1s, delivered in 1975 and 1976. Having seen some ten years of operational service, these aircraft are still technologically on a par with the best available in the West. The SAAF, which was the first export customer for the Mirage F-1, has two versions. No. 3 Squadron at Waterkloof operates the sophisticated all-weather F-1CZ interceptors, while at Hoedspruit No. 1 Squadron has a larger number of the less sophisticated F-1AZs optimized for the ground attack rôle.

The Mirages in the SAAF are armed with a variety of missiles carried on external pylons. Originally the American AIM-9 Sidewinder air-to-air missile armed the Mirage IIICZs, but lately the indigenous infra-red homing Armscor V3B Kukri (externally rather similar in appearance to the Matra R550 Magic, which it will replace in SAAF service) is being phased in for both the Mirage III and F-1. As the Kukri is a relatively short-range weapon, the ageing Matra R530 radar-guided missile may be employed for targets further away. The only armament fitted internally for both the Mirage III and F-1 is a pair of 30 mm DEFA cannons.

In the ground-attack rôle the F-1 makes extensive use of the Matra 155 pod fitted with 18 SNEB unguided missiles of 68 mm calibre. The Mirage IIIEZ utilizes a similar pod known as the Matra JL-100. This pod has a fuel tank in the rear in addition to its missile housing (essentially the same as a Matra 155 pod). If a target demands it, a more sophisticated Nord AS-30 radio-guided air-to-surface missile may be fitted to the centre fuselage pylon of the Mirage IIIEZ.

South Africa does not have a large force of bombers – such aircraft are hardly necessary given the nature of the SAAF's present activities. Most ground-attack missions flown by the SAAF demand little more than unguided missiles such as those fired from the Matra 155 pod. However, a threat from the sea will have to be met by the Hawker Siddeley Buccaneer S Mk 50s of No. 24 Squadron. The SAAF acquired its Buccaneers during 1965 and 1966 in terms of the Anglo-South African Simonstown agreement, and is the only air force other than the RAF to fly the type.

The Buccaneer features four under-wing pylons to which either Nord AS-30 missiles or Matra 155 pods may be fitted, and a rotating integral bomb bay which enables the aircraft to carry four 1 000-pound bombs. Oddly, the maritime strike Buccaneers are based inland at Waterkloof, Pretoria – but an in-flight refuelling capability ensures that the aircraft can operate beyond their normal range. Similarly, as a trade-off against a large, sophisticated radar system (perhaps less important in view of the subcontinent's predominantly favourable weather), the ground-attack Mirage F-1AZs have a retractable air-to-air refuelling probe in the nose for refuelling from a tanker-Buccaneer.

The ageing English Electric Canberra may be regarded as the only other dedicated bomber in the SAAF inventory. In recent times these aircraft have donned an overall blue colour scheme in keeping with their rôle as high-altitude strategic reconnaisance aircraft. In place of bombs in an internal bay, they may be fitted with a camera pack. Under-wing strong points permit light loads (such as Matra 155 pods) to be carried.

The Canberra B(I) Mk. 12s delivered to No. 12 Squadron at Waterkloof in 1963 were constructed from remaining spare components and were the last new Canberras delivered. The Canberra T Mk. 4s were acquired as refurbished second-hand aircraft and are now the oldest jet aircraft in the SAAF inventory, having been built for the RAF in 1953.

The characteristic rasp of the venerable Harvard was a familiar sound for some 40 years at flying schools around South Africa. Today, after most air forces have retired these aircraft, they still drone around the circuit at Dunnottar's Central Flying School – home of the world's largest concentration of Harvards. The SAAF has become the largest military operator of Harvards – and probably the last.

A milestone in South Africa's aviation history was the advent of the locally manufactured Impala jet trainer. The manufacturing licence obtained by Atlas Aircraft Corporation served as a foundation on which South Africa could build its own aircraft industry – an industry on which it might have to rely heavily in the future.

The MB326M Impala Mk. 1 is the South African derivative of the Italian Aermacchi MB326 jet trainer. The first Impalas, which replaced the SAAF's ageing Vampires, were obtained directly from Italy in 1966, followed by further aircraft assembled by Atlas from knocked-down components from the parent factory. As production got under way, more and more local content was introduced, so that by the time production switched to the single-seat MB326KC Impala Mk. 2 in 1974, virtually the entire airframe and motor was of local manufacture.

The Impala Mk. 1's primary rôle is the jet training of fighter-pilots after the initial Harvard phase. Most Impala Mk. 1s are based at Langebaanweg north of Cape Town – home of No. 83 Jet Flying School, of the SAAF's crack aerobatic team the Silver Falcons, and of No. 7 Squadron. At present, No. 8 Squadron at Bloemspruit and No. 4 Squadron at Lanseria are the prime users of the single-seat ground-attack Impala Mk. 2s (although a few Mk. 1s are also flown by these units), with detachments operating permanently from Ondangua in northern Namibia. No. 85 Combat Flying School at Pietersburg also flies the type as air combat trainers.

Both the Impala Mk. 1 and Mk. 2 have six under-wing strong points to which may be fitted a variety of stores in various combinations. Typical Impala ordnance includes combinations of fuel tanks, 30 mm cannon pods, Matra 155 pods, bombs (120 kg or 250 kg) or tactical photo-recce pods. The single-seat Mk. 2 version has added firepower in the form of two integral 30 mm DEFA cannon in the nose.

Although the Impala Mk. 2s which fly counter-insurgency and close air-support missions in the operational area of Namibia contribute materially to the war effort, the helicopters used there play a vital if not decisive rôle. The backbone of the SAAF's helicopter component is the French Sud (later Aerospatiale) Alouette III and the Aerospatiale SA330 Puma.

The Alouette III was introduced into SAAF service as long ago as 1962, progressive deliveries of this versatile seven-seat helicopter making it numerically the largest type. Apart from widespread use in the operational areas, the Alouette IIIs are employed within South Africa by the helicopter units at the coast (No. 22 Squadron at Ysterplaat, No. 16 Squadron at Port Elizabeth and No. 15 Squadron at Durban) and by two helicopter units in the Transvaal (No. 17 Squadron at Swartkop and No. 31 Squadron at Hoedspruit). A large number of Alouettes equip

No. 87 Helicopter Flying School at Bloemspruit, where prospective SAAF helicopter pilots are trained after doing their 'basics' on Harvards.

The SAAF was the first customer outside France to accept delivery (in December 1969) of the Aerospatiale Puma. Like the Alouette, the twin-engined Puma offers excellent versatility. It is capable of lifting 16 fully-equipped troops, and is flown extensively by No. 19 Squadron (headquartered at Swartkop) in combat situations in northern Namibia. The helicopter units within South Africa (Nos 16, 30 and 31 Squadrons) each have a Puma component. Recently the South African Navy fleet replenishment ship SAS *Tafelberg* was converted to a helicopter carrier with hangarage for two Pumas, normally shore-based with No. 30 Squadron at Ysterplaat.

The heaviest helicopter in the SAAF inventory is the three-engined Aerospatiale SA321L Super Frelon, acquired in 1967 and 1968. Even though its spacious interior accommodates larger cargoes or 27 fully-equipped troops, this helicopter has now found more suitable applications with one of the coastal helicopter units, No. 15 Squadron, while the Pumas bear the brunt of combat operations in Namibia. The casual observer might believe the Super Frelon's ship-like hull permits amphibious operation, but in fact the SAAF version is the non-amphibious type (without stabilizing undercarriage sponsons).

The Westland Wasps (procured in batches between 1964 and 1972) are the only helicopters in the SAAF that are not of French origin, and are also South Africa's only helicopters possessing an inherent offensive capability. They were acquired from the United Kingdom as shipboard anti-submarine warfare helicopters for frigates of the South African Navy (they functioned as delivery platforms for two Mk. 44 torpedoes). A change in strategy led to the phasing out of the Navy's frigates, relegating the Wasps to a new primary rôle, that of search and rescue. Until recently home base for the Wasps of No. 22 Squadron was Ysterplaat, but they continue to find useful application as light utility helicopters operating from naval vessels such as the hydrographic survey ship SAS *Protea* and the remaining frigate SAS *President Pretorius*. The Wasps have subsequently joined the Test Flight and Development Centre.

The SAAF plays a major part in patrolling and defending South Africa's long shoreline, but the retirement (without suitable replacement) of the last three Avro Shackletons in November 1984 has somewhat curtailed this side of the SAAF's operations.

In what is seen as an interim measure, No. 35 Squadron at Cape Town's D. F. Malan Airport replaced its Shackletons with radar-equipped Dakotas transferred from No. 80 Air Navigation School, affording the unit a limited patrol and SAR capability. A second-

ary rôle for No. 35 Squadron's Dakotas is the training of the SAAF's navigators.

In addition, the Italian Piaggio P166S Albatrosses of No. 27 Squadron have been responsible since 1969 for the close inshore patrol of the South African coastline, taking over much of the Shackleton's workload in the twilight of the latter's career.

Since the Second World War the venerable Douglas C-47 Dakota has played an important rôle as the backbone of the SAAF's transport capability. The SAAF has the proud distinction of having operated the Dakota continuously since June 1943, when the first of the 'Daks' (supplied in terms of a Commonwealth lend-lease scheme) were delivered to No. 28 Squadron and later to No. 44 Squadron.

However, with the scaling down of air force inventories in the period after the Second World War, many of the SAAF's 84 Dakotas were demobbed, finding their way to civil operators in southern Africa and as far away as Canada and Burma. In recent times, though, the SAAF has again acquired Dakotas – from various sources – and today it is the world's largest operator. Many believe that the 50-year-old workhorse will still be around well into the next century.

SAAF Dakotas flown by aircrew from two transport units – No. 25 Squadron at Ysterplaat and No. 44 Squadron at Swartkop – serve in the operational area of Namibia. Transport pilots are trained to fly multi-engined aircraft using the Dakotas based at No. 86 Multi-Engine Flying School at Bloemspruit. This unit also supplies the Dakotas used for parachute training drops by the South African Army's Parachute Batallion based at Bloemfontein.

Flying alongside the Dakotas of No. 44 Squadron are Douglas DC-4 Skymasters acquired from South African Airways in January 1966. (Interestingly, one of these DC-4s was the last example built.) Normally these four-engined transporters are configured as passenger aircraft, but the large cargo doors also permit other loads to be carried. Recently, a few of the earlier C-54s (a Second World War variant) and a Vickers Viscount (transferred from No. 21 Squadron) joined the fleet of No. 44 Squadron.

The four-engined Lockheed C-130B Hercules and the twin-engined Transall C-160Z (the latter acquired from France in 1969) equip No. 28 Squadron at Waterkloof. They have similar-sized fuselages with a large cargo door in the rear – spacious enough to accommodate cargo as bulky as a Puma helicopter.

The transportation of VIPs is an important task of any air force. To this end, a special unit – No. 21 Squadron at Waterkloof – operates such aircraft as the HS 125-400B Mercurius and Beechcraft King Air 200Cs.

The light aircraft in the SAAF are often forgotten, yet they perform a variety of indispensable tasks. Artillery spotting and forward air control are undertaken by Italian-manufactured Aeritalia-Aermacchi AM3CM Bosboks, whose home base is No. 42 Squadron at Potchefstroom. The Bosboks replaced the Cessna 185s in this rôle from 1973 onwards, relegating the Cessnas to training rôles with No. 84 Light Aircraft Flying School (also at Potchefstroom).

The Atlas C4M Kudu is a South African designed and manufactured general-purpose aircraft, used for tasks such as visual reconnaissance, supply dropping and casualty evacuation, features many components of the Italian Bosbok. No. 41 Squadron at Swartkop is the home base for this versatile eight-seater aircraft.

It is evident that the SAAF is still adequately equipped for all the various tasks demanded of it – both in the peacetime environment within South Africa and in the low-intensity counter-insurgency war being fought in northern Namibia.

The supply of arms to South Africa is a politically sensitive issue that affects both the acquisition of hardware, and more recently, the supply of spares. However, there is no lack of ingenuity – what is unobtainable abroad is simply manufactured locally. Time-expired Puma rotor blades, for example, have now been successfully replaced with locally manufactured equivalents.

With the Impala and Kudu production completed, Atlas is now gearing itself to the production of a locally designed, dedicated combat helicopter.

While there can be no doubt that South Africa has the expertise to produce sophisticated combat aircraft, economic considerations will – for the time being, anyway – inhibit projects of this nature. At present the SAAF knows it must make do with what it has by way of equipment – a challenge it is meeting with a high degree of success. Now, more than ever, it is living up to its motto: *Per aspera ad astra*.

ally anyone can learn the techniques. The materials used – plastics and fibre-glass – provide for fast construction, light weight and structural strength in an airframe of exceptionally 'clean' aerodynamic finish. This has led to aircraft that can achieve 320 km/h in level flight, powered by a Volkswagen beetle engine (modified to meet aircraft safety standards).

At today's prices, a home-built aircraft will cost no more than about R20 000. If one compares this to a new, factory-built aircraft costing over R150 000 (for similar performance), it is obvious why home construction and the EAA have become so popular.

Kits or plans for a great number of designs are now available in the USA. Several of these have found favour in South Africa, the most important – numerically – being the KR-2, designed in 1969 by Ken Rand of the Douglas Aircraft Corporation. The prototype was a single seater powered by a 36 hp 1 200 cc Volkswagen engine, which enabled the aircraft to achieve 241 km/h at sea level. In South Africa there are 90 KR-2s under construction, all of which are the later, two-seat, side-by-side version with a more powerful VW engine.

Of course, not all aviators wish to fly little glass bullets. The EAA also caters for enthusiasts who are nostalgic about earlier aircraft, by having an 'Antique and Classic' and a 'Warbird' section. At Oshkosh one can see formations of virtually every type of 'Warbird', from Harvard trainers to Hawker Sea Furies, as well as the recreational aircraft of yesteryear – all restored to a standard that certainly was never achieved by the factories that originally produced them.

Oshkosh is the mecca for sport aviation enthusiasts – and many of its 'pilgrims' come from this country. It is significant that after the Australians, the next largest foreign contingent to visit Oshkosh in 1984 came from South Africa, which has ten active EAA chapters and its own EAA convention, now held at Margate on the Natal South Coast. About 10 000 people visited the Margate show in 1985 and there were 350 aircraft present, making this the largest sport aviation event outside North America.

The EAA in South Africa had its beginning in Durban and Johannesburg, where activities began almost similtaneously and with the same goals – to fly at an affordable price.

Mike Spence was the first to form an EAA-recognized chapter in South Africa in 1964 (Chapter 322). Like Paul Poberezny, he made a modest start: chapter members met in a garage after work and talked long into the night, standing around an old coffee machine. Spence is the only South African to be elected a life member of the EAA in the United States – a tribute to his foresight, enthusiasm and dedication to sport aviation.

While Spence was busy in Johannesburg, a group of enthusiasts in Pietermaritzburg and Durban had formed an association known as

5

FOR THE LOVE OF FLYING
Recreational aviation

VINTAGE, EXPERIMENTAL AND HOME-BUILT

BY BOB EWING

In 1953 a far-sighted American named Paul Poberezny brought together a group of former service pilots who wanted to continue flying but lacked the wherewithal to do so. These men designed and built their own aircraft, of which the following benefits were readily apparent: low price, low maintenance costs, exclusive design, small size, low storage costs and low running costs.

Because prototype aircraft are classified in the Federal Aviation Regulations as 'experimental', Poberezny's group eventually became known as the Experimental Aircraft Association – or EAA, as it is better known today. From modest beginnings the EAA has grown into a gigantic, worldwide movement with half a million members and over 850 chapter centres. It holds its annual convention and air show at Wittman Field, Oshkosh, Wisconsin in July/August each year. This is now the biggest air show in the world – drawing three quarters of a million spectators and, in 1984, 14 500 aircraft. Many of the aircraft seen at Oshkosh are built using revolutionary construction methods that have been developed to the level where virtu-

the Aircraft Builders' Association, led by Ian Lewis. One of its members was Woody Woods, a former United States Air Force major. He built the first Pitts Special in South Africa – thereby introducing a totally new dimension to aerobatic flying in this country. (He also imported the first Grob motor glider, another breakthrough in light aircraft design.)

Sakkie Halgreen, the chairman of Chapter 844 (based at Lanseria), is undoubtedly the most active exponent of home-building. He owns the agency for the Rand KR-2 kit, discussed above.

With so much enthusiasm and talent around, it soon became obvious that an annual convention was needed – a meeting at which all the enthusiasts could gather to show off their aircraft (and their prowess) and enjoy the camaraderie of their fellows.

The first EAA convention in South Africa was held in Pietermaritzburg in 1972, followed by a second in Springs in 1973 and another in Welkom the following year. In 1975 the show moved to Swinburne (for two years), then to Allemanskraal at the Willem Pretorius Game Reserve. It moved back to Swinburne in 1977 and 1978, then to Mkuze in 1979 and 1980 – where the National Aerobatic Championships have been held for the past few years.

By this time the EAA Convention had become the main event of the year for enthusiasts, and the date around which they planned their building programmes and flying holidays. Because of their ever-increasing numbers, a larger, more sophisticated venue was sought, and Margate was finally selected because of its ideal facilities and support infrastructure.

The following are just some of the interesting home-builts that have visited the Margate convention or are under construction in South Africa:

The Bakeng Duce, built from conventional materials such as wood, fabric and steel tubing, is known as a 'parasol monoplane'. It accommodates two persons in tandem in open cockpits and cruises at about 225 km/h. The only flying example in South Africa was built and is owned by Courtney Jane of Brakpan.

The Thorpe T18, known as the T18 Tiger, is an all-metal construction. Two of these aircraft are based at Virginia Airport, Durban.

The Taylor Titch, a beautiful single-seat sport monoplane, was designed by John F. Taylor in the UK. His aim was to produce an all-wood and fabric airframe costing no more than £100. Of the Titches in South Africa, perhaps the most impressive-looking is the one owned by 'Fluffy' McKerchar, an SAA flight engineer who regularly demonstrates this aircraft's aerobatic agility at airshows around the country.

The Pitts Special, developed from its original 90 hp configuration to over 200 hp, has become the yardstick against which aerobatic performance is measured. The Winfield Cig-arette Company currently sponsors a team of three Pitts Specials in South Africa.

A flying example of an Evans VP1 is owned by Barry Hogarth of Durban. This aircraft is ideal for the novice home-builder and sacrifices appearance and performance to achieve ease of construction. Built largely from wood and fabric, it is a strut-braced low-wing monoplane. The original design used a 40 hp VW engine, but later versions have more powerful VW engines and fly at about 190 km/h at sea level.

The Pietenpol Aircamper was one of the very first home-built designs, developed by Bernie Pietenpol in 1933 using a 40 hp Model A Ford engine. A two-seat parasol monoplane, it is built from Sitka spruce, fabric and metal tubing. With bungee undercarriage, tailskid and disc wheels, it is a classic home-built aircraft. Fifteen are currently under construction in South Africa and it is hoped that the first one will take to the air in 1986.

Home-building does not stop at new designs: many derelict and rotting hulks have been resurrected and restored to their former splendour. After the Second World War the RAF in Southern Rhodesia sold its de Havilland DH82A Tiger Moth trainers to the SAAF, and in the 1950s these were again sold – this time to the public as scrap. Many were bought for as little as £5 and broken up. Sometimes only the engines were kept and used as water-pump motors on farms. The better aircraft could be flown away for £10-£15. Over 9 000 Tigers were built, of which about 40 survive in this country.

The name Bok Strecker has become inextricably linked with South Africa's restored Tiger Moths. Strecker, who was personally trained as a de Havilland engineer by Geoffrey de Havilland at Baragwanath Airfield back in the 1930s, has a licence bearing the number 18 – an indication of his vintage. Nearly all South Africa's beautifully restored Tiger Moths owe their existence to the reverent touch of Bok Strecker and his family.

Another important vintage aircraft to have flown in South Africa was the writer's Beech Staggerwing, which had previously served as the personal transport of Prince Bernhard of the Netherlands during the Second World War. This classic biplane has now been sold back to the USA, the new owner (an EAA member) living in Wichita, Kansas – the birthplace of the Staggerwing. Only one other example of this aircraft survives in South Africa – in Clocolan in the Orange Free State.

The restoration bug has even bitten the SAAF and SAA. The SAAF Museum boasts one of the world's best collections of rare and special aircraft, which are regularly flown for the public. The queen of these is undoubtedly the Spitfire *Evelyn*, a world famous aircraft rebuilt by its owner Larry Barnett, Alan Lurie and other dedicated enthusiasts.

SAA recently restored its magnificent Junkers Ju52/3m to flying condition, deck-ing it in the authentic colours of the period. This plane now thrills people around the country with its mighty radial-engined roar.

With the wealth of knowledge and material available from overseas – particularly from the USA – and the enthusiasm of South Africa's 800 EAA members, the future of sport aviation in this country seems assured. A visit to Margate is enough to fill any enthusiast with the desire to build and fly his own aircraft at a price he can afford. Grass roots aviation in South Africa is alive and well.

AEROBATICS

BY CHRIS MARAIS

Aerobatic competition flying is a solo exercise, the pilot and his aircraft engaged in 'pushing the envelope' to its maximum across a 1 000-metre 'box' of sky and performing an intricate aerial ballet that looks impossible from the ground.

The excitement generated within the pilots does not start only once the craft is airborne. Explains Brian Zeederberg, four times South African aerobatic champion and currently the world champion Tiger Moth aerobatic pilot: 'Often, the pilots are so full of adrenalin before a competition that they become too wound up to fly. In effect they have peaked too early. You can see the nervous ones on the airstrip even before they take off.'

Pilots have a solid meal before taking off to perform a 12-minute sequence involving 25 manoeuvres. The food provides better 'G tolerance' while flying.

In his confined 'box' of air, the aerobatic pilot finds himself facing two opponents: the other competitor and himself. At 300 km/h the blood drains away from the top half of the body (this is known as the positive G syndrome). One of the other symptoms of this phenomenon is what pilots call 'tunnel vision'. Negative Gs, on the other hand, cause a rush of blood to the head. 'That's when your head feels the size of four footballs', says Zeederberg.

Brian Zeederberg and his associates do practise mostly at Syferfontein in the Transvaal. This is regarded as the centre of South African aerobatics, and it was near there that Zeederberg nearly died when he crashed his Pitts into an ant hill at 190 km/h.

Like many of his contemporaries, Zeederberg acquired his love of flying through his father's influence. 'When I was a child, my father used to repair various aircraft and I would always be around, roller skating about the hangar.' In 1965 he realized his dreams and began flying. Today he has over 2 000 flying hours to his credit and is proficient on 140 different aircraft. 'Because I taught myself aerobatic flying in a Tiger Moth, all the initial imperfections showed up – the Moth is that type of flier.'

When Zeederberg took over the South African Aerobatic Club in 1979, one of its major problems was the lack of aircraft for training. 'It's very expensive. In effect you have to put your money where your mouth is before you even know if you like aerobatic flying.'

A two-seater Pitts Special costs upwards of US$70 000 – more than R200 000 at 1985 rates. There are currently nine Pitts specials in operation in South Africa. Other great aerobatic aircraft are made by Zlin (a Czechoslovakian airplane) and Yak, a Russian manufacturer. There are only five Zlin 50s in the West, one of which is owned by South African aerobatics ace Peter Celliers.

Aerobatic competition is a physically demanding activity, and one which does not permit mistakes. There is a sign above Brian Zeederberg's desk which reads: 'Aviation in itself is not inherently dangerous. But to an even greater degree than the sea, it is terribly unforgiving of any carelessness, incapacity or neglect.'

But there is another, more 'laid-back' aspect to aerobatics: formation flying. This is where Scully Levin and his Winfield Magnum team come into focus. In their bright red livery the three Pitts Specials in this team have been skimming through the South African skies since the middle of 1985. In perfect harmony, Scully Levin, Jeff Birch and Chris Rademan ease their way through beautiful manoeuvres such as the 'switchblade', the 'barrel roll' and the daring 'chicken run' – in which two of the Pitts appear to be on a collision course.

The three men are pilots with SAA, and formation flying has become their after-hours passion. They often practise outside Parys in the Orange Free State because the air traffic in that area allows them comparative freedom of movement. In addition, the local airfield has all the facilities and on-the-spot technicians they could require in case repairs are needed at the last minute.

Scully Levin, who is credited with the rejuvenation of South African aerobatics in the early 1970s, doesn't mind the more sedate form of 'sky dancing'. He says: 'Solo aerobatic competition requires a lot of time and devotion. My SAA job doesn't allow me to spend that amount of time on the sport.'

Three Pitts flying overhead in formation is far more dramatic and appears more dangerous than a solo performance. There is a touch of illusion to formation flying: the aircraft look almost as if they are touching. In the 'bomb-burst' manoeuvre, the three Pitts peel out like the petals of a flower after what seems to the spectator on the ground to be a very near miss. But this is sheer theatre, really – there is no competition.

Scully Levin became widely known for his ability to land his Piper J3 Cub on the back of a moving truck – one of the routines he performed to build up his reputation. He would often be seen at country airshows waving to the crowds from his cockpit and clearly having as much fun as the people on the ground. His aviation career has spanned more than two decades, during which he has won the South African National Aerobatic Championships three times.

The current South African aerobatic champion in the 'unlimited' category, Peter Celliers, was responsible for organizing the most significant aerobatic event ever to take place in South Africa – the South African World Aerobatic Masters Tournament, held at La Mercy airstrip near Durban in October 1985. With 24 competitors from 14 different countries, this was one of the largest shows of its kind ever held. Owing to the last-minute withdrawal of the event's sponsor, Celliers underwrote the tournament himself – to the extent of almost R1 000 000! The winner was Eric Muller of Switzerland, with Kermit Weeks of the USA in second place followed by Manfred Strössenreuther of Germany. Of the three South Africans who took part, André van Kraayenburg and Celliers himself were placed in the top ten, with Brian Zeederberg in 14th position – a considerable achievement when one considers that there are only about 35 active aerobatic pilots in this country. The tournament was so successful that Celliers hopes to stage a similar event in South Africa every three years.

Following a slump in the sport, aerobatics in South Africa is undergoing a resurgence of activity and interest – a trend that will undoubtedly be sustained by an event such as the Masters Tournament at La Mercy. But because of the cost of the aircraft involved, aerobatics in this country – as elsewhere – will inevitably remain the preserve of a small but elite band of skilled flyers who operate at the cutting edge of modern piston-engined aviation and who regard their sport as the ultimate form of private flying.

GLIDING

BY ANN AND TED RUDNICK

*T*he history of gliding in South Africa goes back at least as far as 1875, when Mr Goodman Household built and flew a glider in Karkloof, Natal. Beyond this bare fact nothing much is known – except that two generations of his descendants are still gliding happily most weekends. Rather better known are the exploits of S. W. Vine, the chauffeur-mechanic of the then Governor-General, who in 1912 designed and built a hang-glider in which he made a remarkable number of flights – on one occasion staying aloft for about a mile. In the early 1930s the same man built the well-known Avis sailplane, whose tally of successful soaring flights included one (in 1936) of over five hours' duration. In the same year Philip Wills of Britain, the father of modern gliding, completed South Africa's first cross-country flight when he travelled from Quaggapoort, in the Magaliesberg mountains near Pretoria, to Rand Airport.

That year – 1936 – was a significant one for South African gliding. During the preceding period, clubs had been established in many parts of the Union of South Africa and South-West Africa, and the records show that in this year the D.C.A. (Directorate of Civil Aviation) vested control of gliding activities in the South African Gliding Association. The first 'C' Badge was registered that year (1985 saw the award of 'C' Badge No. 1500).

The tally of achievements continued to grow. In 1949 Boet Dommisse stayed aloft for 9 hours and 18 minutes – a feat of endurance still unchallenged. In fact, the record is no longer in danger: duration record bids subsequently lost favour and the emphasis of competition flying shifted to distance attempts. At first these consisted of straight-line flights – very unpopular with retrieving crews whose task it was to fetch both pilot and craft back to base in time for the next day's flying. This was especially relevant when the distance flown came close to Brian Steven's unbroken 1963 record – 618 km from Baragwanath to De Aar.

In recent years the threat that constantly-improving glider performance would lead to ever longer and less practical distances being flown, has necessitated yet another change in the pattern of competition flying – this time to a more manageable 'task' flown around fixed points and returning to base, with performance related to average speed achieved.

The gliding movement in South Africa has maintained close and fruitful links with similar organizations overseas. The meteorological conditions in this country, allied to a wide diversity of terrain, make it a glider pilot's paradise. From the very earliest days this fact was recognized and eagerly exploited, and year after year the pilgrims lugged their gliders from hemisphere to hemisphere, forsaking the winter chills of Europe to try and break their own national and world records in the obliging skies over Vryburg, Welkom, the slopes of the Drakensberg or the sands of Bitterwasse.

Literally dozens of world and national records have been established in South Africa over the years, and distances of 1 000 km and average speeds of the order of 150 km/h have been achieved. The majority of these visitors come from Britain, Germany, France, Holland and Switzerland. Their pilgrimages, and those of Springbok pilots competing in world events, ensure a constant two-way flow of up-to-date information, research results and even aircraft. This enables the various centres of the movement in this country to muster technical expertise and equipment equal to that available anywhere in the world.

In fact, the type of activity that evolved from the early flights relies rather more on the application of sophisticated techniques and sober research than do the more recent (and in the opinion of 'legit' glider pilots, more frivolous) developments in the recreational realms of flight – hang gliding and microlighting. Glider training is a serious and safety-conscious course of practical and theoretical study with stringently-applied and very demanding disciplines. The glider pilot maintains that the practice of the expertise so acquired adds immeasurably to his enjoyment.

The majority of individuals involved in gliding experience their greatest pleasure in the actual practice of the skill, but there are also those who spend their happiest hours at the drawing board and the workbench. World-renowned among the latter is South Africa's Pat Beatty who, at first with Fritz Johl and in later years on his own, has produced no fewer than seven generations of incredibly innovative high-performance gliders. Each of these – in spite of their world-class rating – has been for Pat just one more step towards the cherished goal of the ultimately perfect glider.

The typical high-performance glider of today is a moulded glass-fibre shell, as sleekly aerodynamic as possible, built to hold one or two persons. It is semi-aerobatic with a stalling speed of 60 km/h and a maximum safe speed of 250 km/h, and capable of undertaking loops, spins, chandelles and stall-turns. Equipped with oxygen, radio and a wide range of sophisticated and sensitive instruments to record speed, drift and rate of climb in thermal currents, it is fully able to cope with the constantly extending performance horizons of today's competitive flying. Landing in small fields far from home is frequently an aim rather than a setback for the glider pilot, and his craft is fitted with airbrakes and flaps to facilitate this exercise.

A gliding club may possess the most luxurious of clubhouses with swimming-pool and all conveniences, or nothing but a windsock, a beach umbrella and an earnest soul with a clip-boarded time sheet – but all are rich in enthusiasm, co-operation and a healthy love and respect for the air and its demands. Club officials – instructors, tug pilots and controllers – are members who, having passed demanding tests to attain their ratings, serve according to a roster on an honorary basis.

Normal weekend club flying consists of flights undertaken within a safe gliding distance of the airfield, often with a training programme running concurrently. More experienced pilots, and those owning their own craft (perhaps in a syndicate with others), may venture on cross-country flights involving the possibility of an 'outlanding'.

Once a year (in December) the South African National Championships draws participants from all over the country and Europe to Vryburg's gently undulating semi-desert, which breeds a daily crop of superb thermals – huge columns of rising hot air forging 'stairways' to high altitudes. The gliders spiral upwards until they reach the height from which they can set off across country to the first turn-point of that day's set 'task', using thermals encountered en route as springboards to launch them further along their way. At the airfield there is a network of earthbound specialists – meteorologists, whose calculations prescribe the nature of each day's tasks; pilots of the tug aircraft that tow the gliders up; organizers; timekeepers; runway marshals; radio operators; task-setters; starter marshals; caterers; crews – all of whom make it possible for the pilots to slip their earthly bonds, and soar.

MICROLIGHTS

BY ALAN BLAIN

Asked to describe the sensation of flying a microlight, an enthusiast might reply: 'It's like riding a bicycle 300 metres above the ground'. Despite its appearance, the sport is not dangerous: between 1979 and August 1985 only six people had been fatally injured in microlight aircraft accidents in South Africa. Say exponents of this fast-growing pastime: 'Considering that every weekend hundreds of aircraft are flying hundreds of hours all over the country, that is a remarkable achievement – especially when one considers that during the first five years of the sport's existence, pilots were mostly self-taught or at best given a brief lecture from someone who was self-taught. We should therefore bury the 'unsafe' misconception and get on with the thrill of microlight flight.'

Microlight pilots are drawn from every walk of life. They might include a bank-clerk, farm manager, millionaire property tycoon, air-hostess, printer, doctor, airline pilot and even a former Spitfire pilot. Says a convert: 'The most satisfying thing is seeing all these people at some open dusty airfield, indulging in the modern-day version of what pilots refer to as hanger talk. They share a common love, the camaraderie of facing the same elements, the pride and warmth of belonging to a group who have come as close to natural flight as possible.'

The dizzy spiral of competition that made light aircraft more complex, more sophisticated and more expensive has led to a huge pool of people anxious to fly – but unable to afford it. In addition, say microlight advocates, repairs, spares, constant inspections, hangarage, insurance and fuel costs take much of the pleasure out of flying conventional light aircraft. Moreover, sitting in a totally-enclosed air-conditioned and relatively noiseless cockpit does not bear comparision with the exhilarating immediacy of microlight flight.

A microlight enthusiast describes a typical outing: 'Peering out of the window into the pre-dawn gloom, you see a calm and inviting sky. After dressing warmly you quietly leave the house and hitch the trailor – on which your microlight is perched – to your car. Minutes later you are at the field. Fifteen minutes later your aircraft is rigged, the pre-flight inspection is complete and the engine has been fired up. You line up at the end of the runway, and as the sun bursts into the new day you gun the engine to maximum. The first sensation is that of sudden acceleration as the wind rushes into your face and the noise rises in tempo with your adrenalin. The ground is so close you can touch it as you glide along the runway. Slowly you ease back on the stick and you are airborne, climbing up to meet the rising sun.

'As you gain altitude your horizon increases in magnitude, and you feel master of all below you. You become acutely aware of the change in your perspective as buildings, roads, streams, fields and a variety of places you never knew existed pass below you. And all the time you're moving through the air at a sedate and stately 60-80 km/h. The further the earth drops away from you, the slower you seem to be moving, until eventually you appear to be stationary, hanging suspended in your airborne armchair. And all this for an operating cost of only R35 an hour.'

One of the many people who have experienced the invigorating pleasure of microlight flight is a Karoo farmer who used his micro to check his flocks, but couldn't always find a sufficiently large landing field. Simple ingenuity resulted in the farm bakkie being converted into a mobile airfield. After briefing the senior farmhand in the finer points of mobile airfield operation, the pilot-farmer practised with a few dry runs – and his problem was solved. He could now land virtually anywhere.

Microlights had their origins in the United States in the 1960s, when aviators were trying to get delta-wing bamboo and plastic hang-gliders to fly. They could be seen running down hills or dunes on any sunny and windy day, trying to coax these primitive hang-gliders into the air. The first flights in those days took the pilots no more than 7-14 metres and could be attributed more to the contours of the launch area than the craft's aerodynamic efficiency. Flights inevitably ended in bruised knees, scrapes and scratches and – in some cases – severe or fatal injuries.

After a while, however, the pilots learned to control their mounts. Once these pioneers experienced the thrill of staying airborne, they used aluminium and synthetic sail fabrics to improve their craft. This was the start of modern ultralight construction. Soon the flights lengthened in duration and distance, and pilots could now achieve lift by harnessing thermals or wind. But most flights ended with more bruises and the inevitable trudge back up the hill.

It was at this point that pure hang-gliding and what has grown into microlight flight, parted company. Some of the less physically robust pioneers, considering the advantages of powering their crude hang-gliders, could be seen running through large fields with small motors fitted with propellers strapped to their backs. As both arms were required to hold the hang-glider wing, the fuel throttle was no more than a tube in the mouth: biting down on it reduced fuel flow and power.

Then someone recalled that wings of a certain shape had been used successfully in flying for many decades, and work began on a conventional wing construction. After a measure of success, using the 'run-and-launch, short flight and pain' method, it was decided to add wheels. The result was the first true ultralight: a wing, a basic undercarriage and a small 2-stroke motor. Engine failure was a real hazard in those early days, but the ardent devotees pressed on.

By about 1976 South African pilots were running in grass fields much like their American counterparts. By 1979 a man named George Keely had flown a Fledge microlight from Durban to Cape Town. The aircraft now sported belt-driven reduction drives, more robust undercarriages, highly efficient wing sections and even a hand throttle. Control was provided by a combination of weight shift and the movement of wing surfaces to spoil or enhance lift. In 1980 Alan Elston (a former SAAF pilot) toured South Africa in a Quicksilver MX, introducing an amused yet enthralled public to microlight aviation. Q-Tech – a small company owned by Anton Zeeman and Fanie van Rensburg – started selling Eagles in 1981. Local manufacture began with Colin Liddle building Grasshoppers and John Young building XCRs.

In 1981 these early aficionados formed an association called MLASA (Micro-Light Association of South Africa). They gathered at a field called Eagles' Nest, north of Pretoria, for their first annual general meeting. At this stage the local authorities had some vague rules for microlight pilots, and appeared to consider the whole thing a fleeting yet troublesome fad. But the numbers of enthusiasts increased and new models appeared. Soon the senior 'microlighters' and the authorities were discussing subjects such as structure, regulations and self-control. In 1982 MLASA joined the Aero Club and became MISASA – the Microlight Section of the Aero Club of South Africa.

Senior committee members began drafting proposed legislation for microlight pilots, while the authorities worked on construction standards for the aircraft. By March 1984 South Africa was a world leader in this field. Microlights were brought closer to the mainstream of civil aviation: pilots needed a licence, aircraft had to be approved before sale to the public, and they also had to be registered. The final stamp of approval, and one of the most far-reaching pieces of legislation, was that 25 hours of the required 40 hours for a private pilot's licence could be flown on a microlight.

Microlight clubs have been formed throughout the country and are flourishing. At the time of writing one of the best examples is the Pretoria Microlight Flying Club, based at Rhino Park, between the city and Bronkhorstspruit – an isolated area where noise doesn't cause problems; dead-flat and free of obstructions. Inaugurated in February 1985, the flying centre has eight runways to cope with varying wind directions, all graded to provide good take-off and landing surfaces. Rhino Park also boasts a coy club-house, lecture and briefing room, and a proliferation of hangars.

Today South Africa boasts a small yet surprisingly robust group of manufacturers. John Young of Microlight Flight Systems in Natal is achieving success with his tandem-seat Shadow Trainer (the first local product to be displayed at Oshkosh). Fanie van Rensburg has switched to local manufacture, and the Basic 4000 – his version of a popular American product he was selling – is in many ways superior to the original. But the most dynamic South African microlight must surely be the Thunderbird Tourer. Louis Meyer of Sport Aviation S.A. has persevered for one-and-a-half years with this aircraft, which has two seats (side by side), ailerons, flaps, a steerable nosewheel, rear-wheel suspension and brakes. It is likely to be the first microlight to rival the Cessna 152s and Piper 140s that have for so long been the mainstay of entry-level training in aviation.

The current exchange rate favours local products and has resulted in strong interest from abroad. Shadows have already been sold to Italy, and orders for other South African products are being placed. In addition, foreign companies are investigating the manufacture of their products in South Africa for export. The microlight industry here come of age, and has proved that it can meet the challenge of supplying an eager flying public.

HANG GLIDING

BY JOHN WILLIAMSON

*H*ang gliding can trace its beginnings to the American space programme: it was the work done in the USA by Dr Francis Rogallo and his wife in their search for a recovery system for space capsules in the late 1940s that led to the discovery of the stable flight characteristics of two shallow semi-cones held in shape by a triangular frame.

The Rogallo wing, as it became known, developed in the 1960s into an aircraft that could be launched, landed, carried and flown under the control of one person. No special landing or take-off areas were required, and it was inexpensive too. The new sport spread rapidly throughout the world.

In 1973 the Rogallo wing was first soared for over an hour. There was much experimentation in these early years, and several pilots were tragically killed. But as a result of accumulated knowledge and experience the aircraft steadily improved in design over the years, and new distance records (225 km) and altitude records (4 175 m) were set. Hang gliders became stronger and safer, and today they are robust, properly designed aircraft built from quality materials and featuring many built-in safety features. The wing is a very light and efficient aerofoil with computer-designed features and made from space-age materials such as mylar – all of which provide a glide ratio in excess of 12:1.

Although the hang glider is continually evolving, each new design is a compromise between weight, ease of rigging and flying characteristics. The next major design innovation is likely to include such additional products of the space age as kevlar, carbon fibre and even ceramics. The use of these light, strong materials is already becoming more prevalent in commercial and military aircraft and motor vehicles.

Hang gliding in South Africa can be traced reasonably accurately to about 1973 and a small group of people that included Herman Pedersen (then 52 years old), Mike Olive and Robbie Robertson. Inspired by developments in the United States and Australia, some of these enthusiasts built their own hang gliders using photographs as plans, while others had access to imported kits. After many trials, not a few errors and considerable (often negative) media interest, hang gliding 'took off' in South Africa.

Clubs were formed and affiliated to the Aero Club of South Africa in 1976, when the Hang Gliding Section was formed to develop the sport and liaise with bodies such as the Directorate of Civil Aviation. This provided a link with the Federation Aviation Internationale through representation on the Commission Internationale de Vol Libre (the International Hang Gliding Committee). South African pilots participated in world championships in 1976, 1983 and 1985 and are presently rated among the ten best in the world.

A simple and effective licensing system – requiring written examinations on subjects such as micrometeorology, glider construction and aerodynamics; the scrutiny of a pilot's log book; and observation by a panel of senior pilots – has existed since 1976. The sport is organized through autonomous clubs in Cape Town, Port Elizabeth, Newcastle, Durban, Pietermaritzburg, Johannesburg and Wilderness. Provincial championships are held each year in the Cape, Natal and Transvaal.

A number of foreign pilots have taken part in the annual National Championships and in the various inter-provincial competitions. All these competitions test flying skills on pylon tasks (flying around a pre-set course of anything up to 100 km or more), cross-country tasks (the pilot who flies the furthest is the winner), and speed tasks to a goal (a specified landing field). Pilots are often in the air for more than eight hours at a time during competitions, and may cover a cross-country distance of more than 200 km.

Hang gliding is a thrilling and relatively cheap form of aviation with few restrictions, open to anyone over the age of 16 who is reasonably fit (though not necessarily super-fit). Says an enthusiast: 'Hang gliding is surely the closest man will get to being a bird. This is pure flight – the air in the pilot's face, his hands on the control bar sensing each ripple in the wind, a gentle swish in his ears accompanied perhaps by the odd squeak from his variometer. Often he will be joined by birds such as eagles, who will fly together with him thousands of metres above the earth.'

The pilot steers his aircraft along ridges, using the lift provided by deflected wind, or he takes advantage of thermals to reach an altitude of 4 000 m and more. His instruments consist only of an altimeter, a variometer (which indicates rate of climb or sink) and perhaps a compass. In his harness he carries a small emergency parachute.

The modern hang glider has evolved from a rather crude and rudimentary wing into a highly efficient and sensitive flying machine. A gigantic advance in design was the Comet, whose automatic variable geometry enabled the wing to change shape automatically in a turn. Other innovations followed. The Firebird dispensed with a king post – thus reducing induced drag – and the South African Valkyrie (based on a UK concept and designed by Dale Lippstreu) introduced a queen post to reduce the drag caused by cross-tubes. The French-designed Azur and Profil did away with the keel pocket.

The most sophisticated hang glider today is probably the French Hermes, which has every conceivable advance built in. With over 30 batons it is a headache to rig and needs constant attention in the air, but once mastered it provides a pilot with the ultimate in free, silent flight.

BALLOONING

BY TERRY ADAMS

Ballooning, man's first successful flight experience, began in France over two centuries ago when the Montgolfier brothers designed and built an 'aerostat' which took two Frenchmen – Jean Francois Pilatre and the Marquis D'Arlandes – on the first aerial voyage.

Southern Africa's ballooning history also goes back a long way. Records show that a French prisoner of war, Christoul Saguerse, wrote to the Governor of the Cape in 1810 requesting permission to launch a 'Globe Aerostatique'. Whether Lord Caledon thought it was all part of an elaborate escape plan is not known, but the request was refused.

Some six years later, in December 1816, Thomas Coussy is reported to have sent a cat up in a balloon, marking the first flight in South Africa. An advertisement in the *Kaapstad's Kourant* of 14 December 1816 described Coussey's plans: 'A balloon 35 feet long and 75 feet in circumference accompanied with a cat, Willi, with due permission, will ascend from the Castle, on Wednesday morning, the 18th instant, at 10 o'clock, weather permitting. Officers of the Garrison will have free admission, but private individuals must be provided with a ticket, signed by the subscriber, which may be had in the upper store of Mr J. de Kok, No. 76 Long Street, price one Rdr. Children will be admitted with tickets at 4 shill. Thomas Coussy.'

Unfortunately the records do not show whether or not Willi made a successful flight.

It was not until almost 70 years later that southern Africa's first balloonist took to the air: he was Major H. Elsdale, a member of Sir Charles Warren's expedition to Bechuanaland. Elsdale made his ascent from Mafeking on 7 April 1885 in a balloon he had transported from the Cape by oxwagon.

A number of balloon acts travelled the country at the end of the last century and during the early 1900s. Among them was Miss Viola Cameron, the first woman to go up in a balloon and descend by parachute (this was in April 1893). The spectators were so impressed by her feats that they took a collection and presented her with material evidence of their admiration.

After 1910, however, there appeared to be little interest in ballooning, and it was only in the 1970s that it became an established sport in many countries. In May 1976, fourteen of the world's best hot-air balloonists from eight countries assembled in Johannesburg to take part in Africa's first balloon race. The race created a great deal of interest, and as a result more and more people discovered that ballooning was an exhilarating and fascinating sport – as well as an excellent advertising medium. It was also found that South Africa's weather conditions compared favourably – in terms of ballooning – with the rest of the world.

The first locally-built balloon took to the air in March 1977. Today there are over 30 South African-designed and constructed balloons, some of which have been exported. Although ballooning in this country started later than elsewhere, the sport is quickly gathering momentum.

The first South African national championships took place in 1977, with four entrants. Today, however, the event draws some 20 balloonists, from whom a team of Springboks is selected to represent the country at the world championships – held every other year. In 1985, some 102 entrants from 24 countries competed, including three from South Africa.

To those who ask what ballooning is all about, one enthusiast replies: 'Firstly, it is freedom – the ability to drift or be suspended in the air with no visible support or hindrance. It is also a way of life: once you are hooked, there *is* no other way.

'It is crawling out of bed before dawn and driving to a rendezvous as the sun starts to rise. It is hard work – carrying, pushing, tugging, unrolling and lifting. It is blackjacks in your socks and cold feet. And then, it is entering a brand new and beautiful world when you are aloft. It is good times and wonderful camaraderie.'

Hot-air balloons float in the atmosphere because they are filled with buoyant gas, produced by burning propane. This gas is contained by the 1 000-plus square metres of colourful nylon fabric which lifts the basket and its occupants skywards. Because balloons are large and colourful, they are admirably suited for use as floating billboards. And it is this advantage that has contributed to the rapid development of ballooning, both in South Africa and other countries.

There are many types of sponsorship, the major form of which is 'corporate identity'. Balloons have also been used very successfully as part of a 'hard sell' campaign, and are a particularly valuable medium in areas where other forms of advertising might be logistically difficult and expensive. Even one flight over a residential area can provide over 50 per cent market penetration and a lasting identification with the product being advertised. The latter point has been emphasized with the introduction of specially shaped balloons. The only limitation to the design of these fascinating aerostats is the amount of money available. Among the different shapes flying today are bottles, houses, castles, faces, monuments, trucks, paint cans, jeans, ice cream cones and even an elephant (complete with howdah). Some of these balloons have made short visits to South Africa, and this year a 'resident' bottle took to the skies.

Another aspect of ballooning which has proved both popular and lucrative is that of taking passengers on 'champagne flights'. The balloons used for this pastime usually carry between six and ten people, and have an envelope capacity of up to 6 000 cubic metres of air.

Balloons vary in price from about R12 000 for a small balloon with a simple design to R30 000 and beyond for a large balloon or one with a very complex design. South Africa is one of only six balloon manufacturing countries (the largest of which is the USA, followed by the UK, France, Japan and Australia) and has exported five of the 30 made to date. It is hoped that more exports will follow – especially in view of the current exchange rates.

Balloon pilots are licensed through the Directorate of Civil Aviation and undergo a strictly supervised course of training with experienced instructors. The sport is administered by the Aero Club of South Africa.

Observers say the future of this small band of aeronauts can only be one of expansion.

Many world records are waiting to be broken in South Africa, they say, and the introduction of small airships may be just around the corner.

SKYDIVING

BY ARI SPANOS

Why would anyone want to jump out of a perfectly serviceable aircraft? The question is inevitable whenever pilots and skydivers meet, and the only possible answer to it is the exhilarating experience of skydiving itself.

There is no doubt that skydivers are a part of the aviation scene, but unlike pilots or even model aircraft enthusiasts, they tend to be technological innocents. Although aircraft are inextricably involved in their sport, they are regarded only as a means of enabling skydivers to enter another dimension – one where man can fly, no matter how briefly.

In 1952 a former Spitfire pilot and member of the Caterpillar Club advertised in the *Natal Witness*, asking anyone interested in parachuting to contact him. His name was Geoff Milborrow. Several people responded, and as a result a military surplus parachute was imported from Britain. It was a 28 ft Irving – a flat, round parachute.

Soon afterwards, a group of aspirant parachutists (led by Milborrow) gathered at Oribi Airport, Pietermaritzburg. With the help of an ex-paratrooper, who taught them the basics of the PLF (Parachute Landing Fall), they set out to make history. Milborrow explains: 'We hired a de Havilland Rapide for the occasion and went up one at a time with the ex-paratrooper. We really didn't have a clue. We had to climb out of a small side door, fight our way on to the wing and grab a strut. Then we just fell off and pulled as soon as we were clear.' Among the other pioneers on that memorable day were Jeff Fredrick, Brian Hill and Neil Joubert.

The Pietermaritzburg Parachute Club was the first of its kind in South Africa, and by all accounts also the first in the British Commonwealth. For a while it was the only club, but then things began to happen in the Transvaal. In 1958 Pat Smith – the man most responsible for the growth of the sport in South Africa – made his first jump at Grand Central Airport. He carried a camera (strapped to his foot) with which to record the event for his newspaper. This was the start of a skydiving career spanning many years and including at least 1 600 jumps. Among his peers, Pat Smith is fondly referred to as 'The General'.

Smith was a dynamic force in the sport in the early days and was responsible for the formation of many clubs other than his own (the Johannesburg Parachute Club). His photographs of skydivers in free-fall promoted parachuting throughout the country. Smith and the late Terence Daly held the first two D licences (the highest rating in skydiving). According to Smith, they flipped a coin to see who would be No. D1: Smith lost.

In the early 1960s the Parachute Section of the Aero Club of South Africa was established, and Pat Smith was among the founding members. The formation of this organization meant that parachuting had become an officially sanctioned sport. It also meant that control was now being exercised over the method of training novices. In 1962 it was decided that for reasons of safety, first-time jumpers would use a static line to open the parachute automatically.

During this time, new equipment began to make its appearance. The 28 ft Irving gave way to the GQ, which had a single section cut-out, giving it forward drive and so making it steerable. This was followed by the TU and the C9 designs, which offered still greater speed and manoeuvrability. In 1964 such high-performance round canopies as the Para Commander and the French Papillon (incorporating the rather radical innovation of lift slots) were introduced. These parachutes were superceded only in the mid 1970s when the Ram-air canopy or 'square' appeared on the scene.

There are presently about 2 000 active skydivers spread among 22 service and civilian clubs in South Africa. More are being trained every weekend – despite the ever-increasing expense – and the sport is active and dynamic.

Parachuting has far transcended its origins. At first the only objective was to ride a parachute to the ground: this in itself was considered quite an achievement. As one enthusiast explains: 'Parachuting consisted of standing on the wing of a Tiger Moth with your hand on the rip-cord, falling backwards, and when the earth came around for the second time, pulling.'

The next step was to find a way of remaining stable while in free-fall. One of the body positions adopted was head down, with the hands behind the back: this position is known as the 'Canerozzo', after its discoverer. Legend has it that he held this position until he could see the rivets on the hangar roof, and only then did he pull his rip-cord.

The so-called Valantin position – face to earth, arms and legs spread – gave the skydiver total control over his body in free-fall. At this point parachuting became skydiving, and these two allied skills of canopy control

and stable free-fall allowed what was once a death or glory pastime to develop into a competitive sport. The first two competitive events were for style and accuracy. Style competition is a series of pre-determined turns and back loops which have to be performed in free-fall. Points are awarded for technique and elapsed time. Accuracy competition, on the other hand, requires a competitor to aim for a 10 cm disc by steering his parachute as skillfully as possible.

Then came RW, or relative work, in which two or more skydivers 'fly' relative to one another, link up and form dynamic patterns in the sky. RW has transformed the sport from one of rather ordinary physical skill into a discipline in which spatial perception and mental attitude are of paramount importance. It has also made team members out of individualists: RW, by its very nature, demands extremely close co-operation.

Over the years it has been refined and improved from wild hit-or-miss baton passes to the present sequential RW competition, requiring four- or eight-man teams to build several different formations on a single jump. The first-ever baton pass in South Africa was made by Bill Waugh and Eugene Le Roux over what is now Krugersdorp Game Reserve in April 1962. But word soon filtered out of the USA that baton passes were 'obsolete', and that link-ups were the thing to strive for. This soon caught on in South Africa, and in 1966 the first three-man star was achieved over Kroonstad by Pat Smith, Bill Waugh and Gavin Walker.

From these beginnings, South Africa has become one of the foremost skydiving nations in the world. The Springbok four- and eight-way RW teams have often won their events or have been placed in the first three against international competition. South Africa has even hosted the World Cup and World Championships.

Although equipment and attitudes have changed radically since the early days, new developments have, ironically, turned skydivers back into parachutists. The advent of the Ram-air canopy has created a new branch of the sport. CRW (canopy relative work) has recently been accepted as a competitive event. Just as RW is the linking up of free-falling skydivers, so CRW is contact between square canopies in flight.

New training methods have made it possible for a novice to perform a free-fall jump on his first time out. The 'accelerated free fall' method of training has been given the green light by the Aero Club of South Africa, and this exciting new facet of the sport is expected to produce a new generation of skydivers to take the sport into the next century.

AVIATION PHOTOGRAPHY

BY HERMAN POTGIETER

Aviation photography can be divided into three categories: ground-to-ground, ground-to-air, and air-to-air. The first category is usually fairly static, and the photographer therefore has to select angles, lenses and parts of the immediate environment to make something special of the aircraft, which may themselves be of help to him if they are particularly pleasing or interesting machines.

Ground-to-air is probably the most difficult category. The photographer is rooted to a spot and the aircraft fly above him or at an oblique angle. Approach speeds are often at hundreds of kilometres an hour, requiring a quick eye and reflexes to keep the aircraft in focus and the subject matter composed, and to select the right moment to trip the shutter. Long lenses are a help if an aircraft is flying some distance away – one can pan and track fairly easily. Head-on passes, however, are more difficult.

Air-to-air is the most exciting. Here the photographer is no longer the only person in the team, but is joined by at least the pilot of the photo plane and the pilot of the aircraft to be photographed. A detailed briefing is imperative before the photo session takes place. During air-to-air photography no deviation should be allowed from the plans made at the briefing; and if an idea does not work it should be abandoned and the photography should move into the next phase. When the session has been completed a few ad hoc photographs may be taken, but only if there is complete understanding about what is needed and also if there is no danger to the aircraft.

I greatly enjoyed taking the photographs for this book, but there were many logistical problems. It is relatively easy to organize the photography of military aircraft – one works through a central authority of SAAF Headquarters and once clearance is obtained a few signals work miracles. In the civilian sector, however, it is far more difficult, although there are some companies and individuals who clearly respect the photographer's craft and operate in a professional way with him. The problem of tracking down the owner/pilot of a civilian aircraft and arranging a photo plane and pilot, was somewhat alleviated at air shows. Here one aircraft could be used to photograph many others, usually in the days preceding a show such as the annual EAA convention at Margate.

Cost was always a problem, especially with South Africa's economy in the doldrums, and most photographs were taken as part of a barter deal involving publicity and so on.

The cameras I used were the old stalwart Nikon F3s I've had for the last five years or so, with the Nikkor 105 mm f2.5 being the main lens for air-to-air photography. I also used the Nikkor 180 mm f2.8 IF-ED and the 300 mm f4.5 IF-ED on many occasions, the latter for ground-to-air shots, as well as the 35 mm f1.4 and the 24 mm f2. In addition, the 18 mm f4 and 16 mm f2.8 fish-eye lenses were extremely good for the remote photography done with Pitts Specials and microlights. I use Fuji 50 and 100 film because I like Fuji's colour saturation and fine grain.

I realized while working on this book that it would be impossible to photograph every type of aircraft operating in South Africa. Because aircraft change hands constantly – some being sold overseas – and because new liveries are frequently applied, it is inevitable that some types have been missed out, particularly among the aircraft of the regional and feeder airlines. Even so, I believe that I have provided a good cross-section of the aircraft currently flying in South Africa.

I have, wherever possible, used air-to-air pictures, on the very simple premise that aircraft were meant to fly and should be photographed doing just that.

1 THE FLYING SPRINGBOK
South African Airways

A South African Airways Boeing 747, with its flaps fully set to 30° for landing, on short finals at Jan Smuts Airport. With flaps thus extended its wing area is increased by some 20 per cent, lift by 80 per cent, enabling the aircraft to fly at slower speeds.

Overleaf: The Boeing 747-344B, with its distinctive extended upper deck, is SAA's pride. ZS-SAU, seen here, was first flown on 27 March 1983 and is one of two of these aircraft – the world's biggest and most expensive airliner, priced at around US $100 million in 1985 – in the SAA fleet. They are used mainly on the long-haul Johannesburg-London service. ZS-SAU is pictured during its descent towards Jan Smuts Airport at the end of a flight from Heathrow.

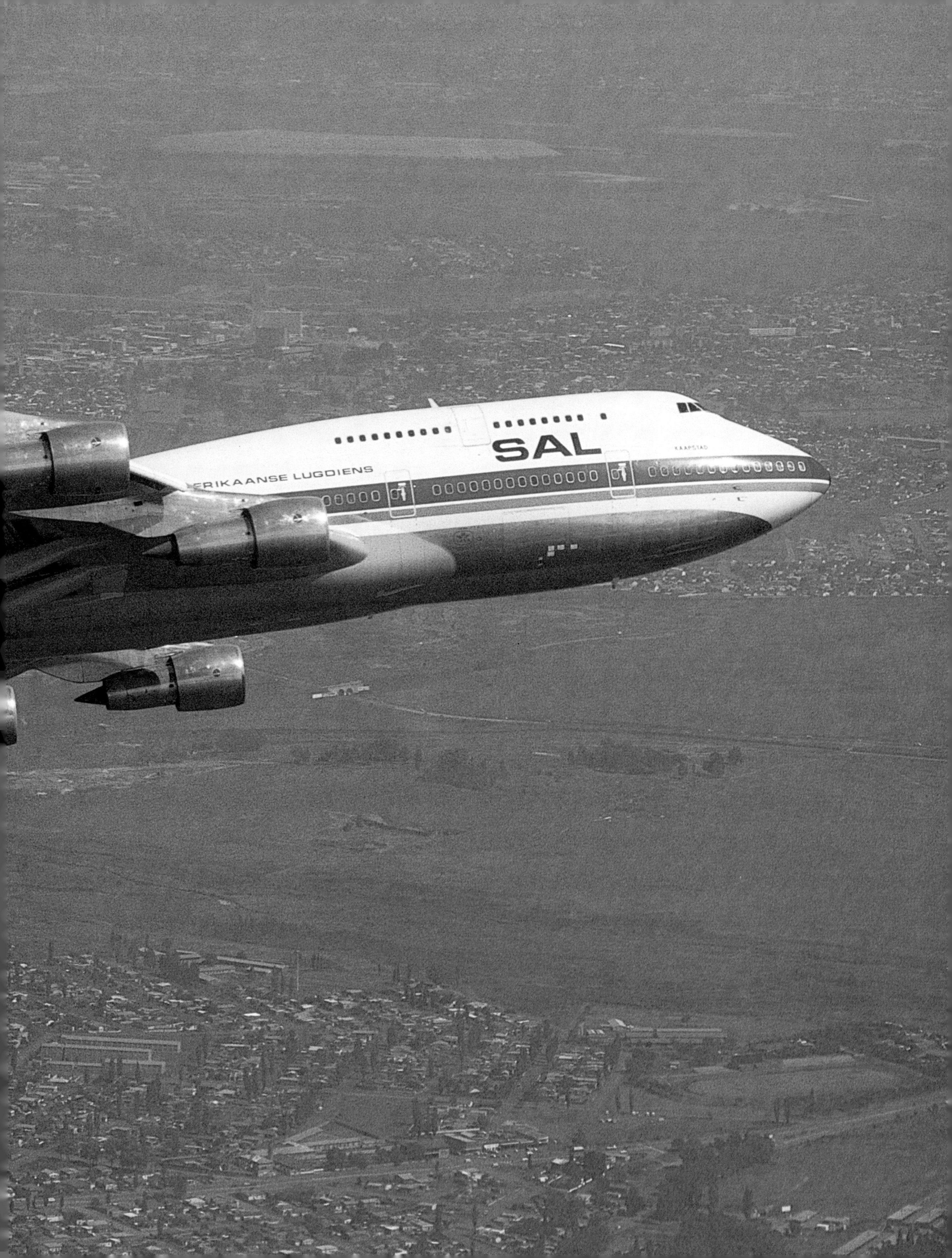
SAL

1 One of South African Airways' earlier Boeing 737-244s, ZS-SBP, takes off from Durban's Louis Botha Airport.

2 The Airbus A300B2K has now seen a decade of service with South African Airways. The first of the aircraft was delivered in November 1976 after SAA had made evaluations of both the Lockheed L-1011 TriStar and the McDonnell-Douglas DC-10. This close-up view shows SAA's second A300B2K – ZS-SDB, *Gemsbok* – taking off from Jan Smuts Airport.

3 With flaps set at 30° and all eighteen wheels lowered, this SAA B747 is seen seconds before touch-down at Jan Smuts Airport. As the First Officer monitors the precise altitude on his radio altimeter, the Captain flares the aircraft by raising the nose a few degrees to slow the rate of descent.

Overleaf: A long-time Boeing operator, SAA showed early faith in the 737 when it ordered six model 737-244s soon after the prototype first flew in March 1967. A further thirteen 737s, all advanced model 737-244(ADV)s joined the fleet in 1981-82 and it is one of these – ZS-SIK, *Olifants* – which is pictured here at about 1 500 ft. over Granger Bay, Cape Town. It is planned to replace SAA's 737 fleet with more fuel-efficient Airbus A320s in the late 1980s.

With its undercarriage about to be retracted, Airbus A300C4-203 – ZS-SDG, *Kudu* – banks over Johannesburg. Clearly seen are the extended leading edge *Krueger* flaps. When SAA ordered its first four Airbuses it specified these high-lift devices for operation from Jan Smuts Airport's hot-and-high conditions. Since then the flaps have become a standard feature of the Airbus. ZS-SDG is SAA's only convertible passenger/freighter Airbus: its cabin can be fitted with various passenger/cargo configurations to suit demand.

1 The German Junkers Ju52/3m formed the backbone of South African Airways' fleet in the 1930s, and all were impressed into SAAF service during the Second World War. None survived the war years. With the establishment of its own historical aircraft collection, one of SAA's prime aims was to acquire its own 'Tante Ju', but the only aircraft of this type were those licence-built, until the early 1950s, by Construcciones Aeronauticas S.A. in Spain and retired by the Spanish Air force in the late 1970s. SAA bought this CASA 352L in May 1981 and restored it to resemble its first Ju52/3m, ZS-AFA, *Jan van Riebeeck*. Here the aircraft flies over the apron at modern-day Jan Smuts Airport.

2 The SAA Museum has two other restored aircraft, albeit not in flying condition. Both the de Havilland DH104 Dove and Lockheed L18-08 Lodestar, here shown against the dark

backcloth of a fire-fighting demonstration, saw SAA service and were bought back by SAA after a spell with several other civilian owners. The Lodestar came from the Aircraft Operating Company, while the Dove was rescued from the scrap-heap at the Biggin Hill aerodrome some miles south of London.

3 The popular three-engined Boeing 727 saw seventeen years' service with SAA when the type was withdrawn in 1982. This 727-44 – ZS-SBE, *Letaba* – achieved some notoriety when, in May 1972, it became the first, and to date only, South African-registered aircraft to be involved in a hijacking. A disgruntled former Anglo American company employee forced its diversion to Blantyre. SAA sold ZS-SBE to Aerotal Colombia in December 1982.

2 THE WIDENING WEB
Regional and feeder airlines

Above: Old Dakotas never die – they just get modernized, like this United Air DC-3, ZS-GPL, complete with updated radar in the nose. The veteran DC-3 – or, more technically accurate, a Long-Beach-built C-47A – was delivered to the United States Army Air Force in May 1943 and, after a post-Second World War spell with American civilian owners, was imported into South Africa in March 1971 by the construction company Grinaker (Pty) Ltd. It became the third DC-3 in United Air's fleet in March 1976.

Opposite page: The Hawker Siddeley HS748 hails from the famed A.V. Roe stable and has been Britain's most successful airliner. A Southern African tour by a company demonstrator in 1970 brought an order for three from South African Airways, who flew these 40-seater aircraft for thirteen years until they were withdrawn on 31 May 1983. Air Cape acquired ZS-JAY, seen here in its new colours over Table Bay, from the French airline Rousseau Aviation early in 1975. This HS748 still comprises the backbone of Air Cape's diverse fleet. Transkei Airways acquired a new HS748 in September 1979, and until recently another had been registered to Protea Airways.

Overleaf: Two Boeing 707s joined Safair Freighters' fleet in October 1985. The aircraft shown here, ZS-LSF, is a model 707-344C, built for South African Airways in 1969 as ZS-SAI, *East London*. It was sold by SAA in March 1979, after which it saw service with a Middle East airline, and more recently with an airline in Europe.

1 The configuration of the Hercules is obviously more functional than aesthetic, and has since become the model for a number of later military transport aircraft. Nevertheless, the civilian L100-30 Hercules cargo carrier pictured here, belonging to Safair and flown by Steve Meyer in a steep bank, shows off its impressive manoeuvrability.

2 Magnum Airlines was the first South African third-level operator to introduce (in 1981) the 18-20 seater Swearingen Metro II. One of Magnum's four Metro IIs is seen here climbing over Johannesburg. Two other airlines, Air Cape and Giyani Airways, each acquired an essentially similar Merlin IVA, both from the South African Air Force, in 1982 and 1984 respectively.

3 The Lockheed L100-30 is the current production version of the civil Hercules and was flown for the first time in 1970. Safair acquired their first Hercules, a shorter-fuselage L100-20, in September 1970 and its first L100-30 late in 1972. Safair eventually became the world's largest operator of civil Hercules aircraft. The airline's striking new livery is displayed here.

1 An historic photograph: on 17 December 1985 the venerable DC-3 celebrated the 50th anniversary of its first flight, when 27 SAAF and civilian DC-3s took part in a formation fly-past over Air Force Base Swartkop. Comair's immaculate DC-3D, ZS-FRM, is seen here taking off on that occasion. ZS-FRM is one of the few DC-3Ds built after the Second World War. It was delivered new to Scandinavian Airlines System on 17 March 1946; Comair bought it from Austrian Airlines in 1969.

2 Although displaying the colours of Mmabatho Air Services – Bophuthatswana's national airline – this Cessna Citation II, ZS-LHW, serves as both Presidential aircraft and ad-hoc charter. Mmabatho's regular airline service, catering mainly for business commuters, is operated by the Brazilian Embraer Bandeirante.

3 Durban-Margate is typical of those short runs undertaken by the kind of small aircraft normally used in the private utility sector. Two of Margate Air's (now Citi Air) six-seater Piper PA-32 Cherokee Six's, a 1974 model (ZS-JGK) and an earlier 1972 model (ZS-MMK), are ideally suited to these routes.

4 The Fokker F-27 Friendship, flown for the first time in November 1955, is the Dutch Fokker company's answer to the perennial problem of finding a worthy replacement for the Dakota, and is still being produced by Fokker-VFW. Comair introduced its first Friendship into service on 31 January 1977 and now has three of the aircraft, all formerly operated by the Australian airline Ansett. ZS-KVJ, in Comair's eye-catching livery, was first flown on 25 November 1964.

3 BUSINESS ON THE WING
Corporate and commercial flying

Left: The Piper PA-31T Cheyenne II is a turboprop development of the earlier, successful, piston-engined Piper Navajo. In this striking study a Cheyenne II, ZS-KTG, is seen flying low over Doornfontein, Johannesburg.

Above: The PA-46 Malibu is one of Piper's latest products. This 1984 model, ZS-LLA — one of the earliest to be built and the first one to be registered outside the United States — is pictured over Virginia Beach, Durban.

Overleaf: The first jet to be registered for business purposes in South Africa was a Learjet 24B — in January 1969. A recent variant of the aircraft is this Swazi-registered Learjet 35A, operated by NAC. Since the type's maiden flight on 7 October 1963, some 1 260 Learjets had been sold by the time the larger Learjet 55 'Longhorn' series was introduced.

1 The Short SC 7 Skyvan was designed as a simple, roomy utility transport capable of lifting a two-ton payload from any half-mile airstrip. Skyvan Series 3, ZS-KMX, seen here in pseudo-military dark-earth colours, was the first to arrive in South Africa. Delivered in February 1981, it and one other of the type are owned by the Ciskei Department of State Security.

2 Appropriately named *Securator*, this Hawker Siddeley HS125-3B/RA – ZS-CAL – was used by the Directorate of Civil Aviation for almost fourteen years to calibrate navigational aids at South Africa's major State airports. It was exported to the United Kingdom in September 1985.

3 Rembrandt Tobacco operates a fleet of four corporate jets – three Dassault-Breguet Falcon 10s and this Falcon 50 – from its home base at Cape Town's D.F. Malan Airport. The Falcon 50's impressive range of 3 500 nautical miles allows one-stop flights between South Africa and Europe.

4 The Cessna Citation is one of the cheaper and quieter business jets on the market, and a very popular one since the first model, a Citation I, was imported into South Africa by Rembrandt Tobacco in August 1975. The insignia on the tail of this Swazi-registered Citation II is that of the Sun International hotel group.

5 The Beechcraft King Air 200 – seen here flying over Johannesburg's central business district – has done remarkably well as a corporate aircraft in Southern Africa.

1

2

3

4

5

1 This near-perfect front view shows the clean lines of a turbo-charged Piper PA-28RT Arrow banking to port over the cane fields near Margate in Natal.

2 Late-afternoon light glows softly on this Piper PA-44 Seminole as it follows a PA-38 Tomahawk in a port break over central Johannesburg.

3 The Piper PA-42 Cheyenne III is currently the flagship of the Piper range of corporate aircraft. It is an enlarged version of the Cheyenne II.

1 Unmistakeably from the same stable, a Beechcraft F33A Bonanza formates with a twin-engined Beechcraft Baron 58. The prototype Bonanza took to the air for the first time on 22 December 1945 and is still being manufactured – one of the longest-lasting in series production.

2 Mike Basson regularly flies the Radio Port Natal sortie in this Cessna 172M Skyhawk, reporting on fishing, surfing, diving, sailing and traffic conditions. Here he banks steeply over the Tugela River.

3 A surrealistic view of aircraft and landscape near Brits in the Transvaal. Types such as this six-seater Beechcraft Baron 58TC are used for ad-hoc charters to points not served by the feeder airlines.

1 Helicopters are in steady demand as crop-sprayers. Here a Bell 47 banks sharply after a low-level run across a plantation.

2 Although the short take-off and landing de Havilland DHC-2 Beaver utility series was designed especially to meet Canadian requirements for a rugged bush aircraft, it has found a wide market the world over. This Beaver, ZS-CAJ, one of two in South Africa, has been with the Department of Transport since March 1959.

3 Aiding the S.A. Kuswag (South African Coast Guard) anti-pollution vessels is this Partenavia P68B observation aircraft, operated by Air Cape and based at D.F. Malan Airport.

1

4 A Piper PA-25 Pawnee releases a full load of insecticide from its hopper. This 1967-model Pawnee, ZS-EXJ, has a 235 hp Lycoming 0-540-B2B5 horizontally opposed piston engine, less than half as powerful as the radial engine of the Thrush Commander shown in the bottom picture.

5 The powerful 600 hp Pratt & Whitney R-1340 radial engine, also used in the well-known Harvard military training aircraft, drives this Rockwell S-2D Thrush Commander, seen spraying, at its operating altitude, near Stellenbosch in the Cape.

3

2

4

5

Helicopters

1

1 An Aerospatiale AS350B Ecureuil (which means 'Squirrel') belonging to Heliquip is silhouetted against the dawn sky as it prepares for an early morning take-off. The six-seater Ecureuil was designed to replace the Alouette III series of helicopters. Heliquip, the South African agents, imported the first in July 1980.

2 Only one Bell 222, a model 222B – ZS-HMD – has so far been imported by Astra Helicopters. The elegant lines of this light, twin-engined ten-seater are clearly seen here.

3 The MBB/Kawasaki BK117, a multi-purpose helicopter, is a joint venture, designed and produced by the Germans and Japanese in tandem. MBB contributed the rotor system, tail unit hydraulic system and power controls; Kawasaki the fuselage, undercarriage and transmission system. BK117A-1 – ZS-HMP – belonging to the Ciskei Government, demonstrates the aircraft's exceptional manoeuvrability with a vertical nose-down attitude after 'bunting' from the hover.

2

1 The Messerschmitt-Bölkow-Blohm BO 105 is probably the most successful product to emerge from the post-Second World War German aerospace industry: it was the first helicopter to achieve world-wide sales without being designed, initially, for military use. In this unusual photograph the BO 105C, ZS-HMJ, and a BK117 do opposing breaks near the Magaliesberg, Transvaal.

2 These two BK117 helicopters, ZS-HMP and ZS-HMY, resemble strike eagles as they 'bunt' in unison.

1 The five-seater MBB BO 105 was the first, and one of the smallest, of the twin-turbine helicopters. Eminently suitable for casualty evacuation and rescue work, it is capable of carrying two stretcher cases, a doctor and an attendant. A South African oil company part-sponsored this BO 105CBS Emergency Medical Service craft. and, although the sponsorship has now been withdrawn, it still performs its vital task – it is based at and operated by the H.F. Verwoerd Hospital in Pretoria.

2 This bird's-eye view of a BK117 clearly shows the helicopter's distinctive twin-turbine engine housing. The first BK117 in South Africa, ZS-HMP, was registered in September 1983, soon after the type began to be distributed world-wide.

3 The closure of the Suez Canal in 1967 presented Autair (and its successor, Court Helicopters) with an excellent opportunity to launch a ship supply service to tankers rounding the Cape of Good Hope. At peak demand a Sikorsky S61N, backed up by a smaller Sikorsky S58ET, were in constant use. Today the service operates from Cape Town and Durban using Sikorsky S58ET twin-turbine helicopters and, in the latter centre, a single-turbine Sikorsky S62A as a standby. The S58ET provides a regular link with oil rigs operating off the southern Cape coast. This S58ET, ZS-HIE, was originally built in the late 1950s as a piston-engined H-34G for the West German Navy and then, in 1979, converted – in Court Helicopters' workshop at D.F. Malan Airport, Cape Town – to a twin-turbine craft.

1 Probably the helicopter with the longest production run, the Bell 47 remained in the parent company's pipeline for 28 years, and for a further two in Italy, where it was produced by Agusta. The excellent all-round visibility afforded by the bubble canopy of this Bell 47 Soloy is clearly evident as it hovers against a backdrop of rocks near Howick Falls, Natal.

2 Since 1983 the beaches of the Cape Peninsula and Durban have been patrolled by Bell 206B Jet Rangers owned and flown by Court Helicopters on behalf of a sponsoring cigarette company. Since the early 1970s Court have operated this popular utility machine for, among other things, electricity powerline patrolling, as a crop-sprayer and, more recently, for sight-seeing tours.

1

2

1 Designed to complement the well-known Alouette III, the five-seater Aerospatiale SA341G Gazelle was the first helicopter to feature the enclosed tail-rotor design, the 'fenestron'. The civil SA341G version of the Gazelle – of which Heliquip's ZS-HYI, shown here, is an example – was the first type authorised to be flown by a single pilot under Instrument Flight Rules (Category I) conditions. No longer used in this rôle, Gazelle ZS-HYI is seen here operating as a 'Trafficopter', providing road situation reports for the commercial radio station Channel 702.

2 Channel 702 also flies this Bell 206B Jet Ranger for its situation reports on the Witwatersrand.

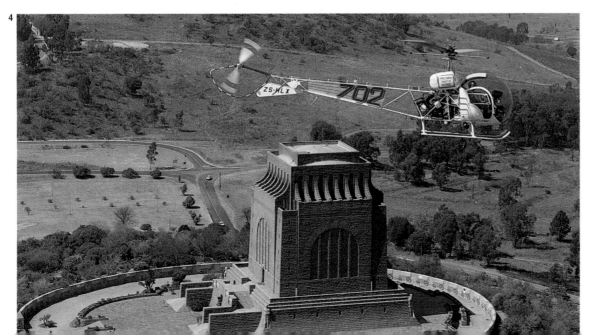

3 Radio Highveld, also using Bell Jet Rangers, pioneered the use of helicopters for traffic reporting. Flying low over Johannesburg's central business district, B206B Jet Ranger ZS-HDZ displays the eye-catching colour scheme and logo of Radio Highveld.

4 The Voortrekker Monument, south of Pretoria, provides an impressive backdrop for an ex-British Army Air Corps Bell 47 Sioux, which supplied the Channel 702 traffic reports until problems with the city's administration caused the service to be suspended.

73

1 The twin-seat RotorWay Scorpion Too is – in most instances – produced from kits supplied to amateur constructors.

2 The skill and enthusiasm of aircraft designer and constructor Carl van Aswegen of Plettenberg Bay are almost unrivalled in South Africa. His first design was a fixed-wing aircraft named Bergwind (ZS-UIS), soon followed by a second fixed-wing, Vansin (ZS-UJT). Carl then designed and built a helicopter, ZS-UTS, which he named Carlsin. His latest creation, ZS-VJX – seen here – is designated Carlsin II and was registered in 1985.

3 Launched in 1980, the two-seat RotorWay Scorpion Exec is very similar to, and superceded, the Scorpion Too. Principal improvements are the pod and boom fuselage.

4 The two-seat Robinson R22 is probably the cheapest factory-produced helicopter available, costing about the same as a four-seat light plane. It is quite popular in South Africa, and there are tentative plans to use it for counting and capturing game.

5 The Hughes H369E, marketed as the Hughes 500, is a light, single-turbine-powered helicopter seating up to six persons.

6 Originally developed for the US Army as a twin-seat training helicopter in the mid-1950s, the civilian Hughes 269 and its three-seat successor the Hughes 300 have been produced in large numbers since deliveries began in 1961. The Hughes 300 is among the most common civil helicopters in South Africa, ranking with the Jet Ranger and the Bell 47. The economical piston-engined machine is eminently suitable for training purposes, but is also widely used in the game management field.

1

2

3

4

5

6

4 CASTLE IN THE SKY
The South African Air Force

Left: Although delivered in the early 1960s, No. 2 'Cheetah' Squadron's Mirage IIICZs remain a front-line interceptor in SAAF service, defending Eastern Transvaal air space from their base at Hoedspruit. No. 800, the first Mirage IIICZ to arrive, is seen here in a high-speed power climb. It is armed with the South African-designed and manufactured Armscor V3B Kukri air-to-air missile.

Above: Close-up of a superb strike fighter: a Mirage F-1AZ from No. 1 Squadron rolls to the right, just past the Puma helicopter camera platform.

1 A Mirage F-1AZ of No. 1 Squadron, Hoedspruit, extends its airbrakes, slats and flaps, so reducing its speed to about 170 knots as it closes in to be photographed from a Puma helicopter. The large long-range ventral fuel tank and four under-wing weapon pylons are clearly visible as the aircraft flies over a cloud-covered Lowveld at a height of around 10 000 ft.

2 A small number of Mirage IIIR2Z tactical reconnaissance aircraft, equipped with the more powerful SNECMA-Atar 09K-50 turbojet, was added to No. 2 Squadron's inventory during the early 1970s. Here a IIIR2Z, No. 854, is seen during a roll, with two external fuel tanks, capable of being jettisoned in flight, protruding from beneath its delta wings.

3 A fully loaded Buccaneer is about as heavy as the Viscount airliner featured on page 89. This underside view of one of No. 24 Squadron's Buccaneer S Mk. 50s shows the open rotating bomb-bay. The Buccaneer has two powerful Rolls-Royce Spey turbofans, a power plant originally developed for such civil airliners as the BAC 1-11 and Hawker Siddeley Trident.

1

2

3

1 More and more air forces are applying low-visibility camouflage to their interceptors – shades of blue are far more effective in the high-altitude environment in which these aircraft operate. This Mirage F-1CZ, No. 203, seen taking off from Ysterplaat on 30 January 1982, was the first SAAF Mirage to appear in the three-tone blue scheme shown.

2 Trailing smoke and flame, unguided SNEB rockets from an SAAF Impala Mk. 2 streak earthwards.

3 The rounded contours of an effective attack aircraft: the starboard 30 mm DEFA cannon lurks menacingly in this head-on view of an Impala Mk. 2 flying high over the operational area in Namibia.

2

3

1 The Silver Falcons, flying Impala Mk. 1s, have been the SAAF's aerobatic team since 1968. The team currently comprises four aircraft (repainted in 1985 in the striking colours displayed in the picture). Here the aircraft climb in perfect line-abreast formation against a Cape Flats backdrop.

2 A pair of Impala Mk. 2s, their olive drab and dark earth camouflage blending well with the dun background of Ovambo countryside, fly at low level after taking off from Ondangua, one of the main operational bases in northern Namibia.

3 An Impala Mk. 2, armed with rocket pods and equipped with auxiliary fuel tanks, flies at extreme low level over Lake Liambezi, near Katima Mulilo. Production under licence by Atlas enabled the SAAF to become the largest operator of the single-seat MB326K version.

1

2

3

1 Graceful Canberras from No. 12 Squadron perform a fighter-style break to port. Closest to the camera is a T Mk. 4 trainer variant of this 1944 bomber design; the other three are B(I)12 interdictors.

2 The SAAF was an early customer for the Hercules, now flown by no fewer than fifty of the world's air arms. The Hercules is still in production more than thirty years after the type's maiden flight on 23 August 1954.

3 The South African Air Force is now the largest operator of the venerable C-47 Dakota. Here a No. 44 Squadron Dak takes off from a forward base in the Northern Namibia operational area.

Overleaf: Only Daks, it is said, can replace Daks – a cliché but nevertheless valid in so many instances. They have even taken over from more modern aircraft. For instance this Dakota, No. 6829, formerly of No. 25 Squadron and seen at low level over the Oudekraal area of the Cape Peninsula, is now part of No. 35 Squadron, flying maritime reconnaissance missions originally performed by Shackletons. It was built at the Douglas Oklahoma City plant in 1943; the SAAF acquired it on 12 March 1944 under the Second World War lend-lease scheme.

1 A full load of paratroopers is dropped from a Transall C-160Z during late-afternoon operations in Namibia. These Franco-German aircraft, together with the C 130B Hercules, make up No. 28 Squadron's complement.

2 A foursome of noisy Piaggio P166S Albatross coastal patrol aircraft struggle to keep line-abreast formation over Cape Town during a strong south-easter wind. Ironically, when delivered to No. 27 Squadron, they took over from Dakotas as close inshore patrol aircraft, but with the retirement of the Shackletons and their replacement once again by Dakotas, the Albatrosses now bear the bulk of the coastal patrol activities along South Africa's lengthy shoreline.

3 A Hawker Siddeley HS125-400B Mercurius overshoots as No. 44 Squadron's sole Viscount clears the runway at Swartkop. The Mercurius had been the SAAF's standard VIP transport until other biz-jets were added to No. 21 Squadron's inventory. Low utilisation means that the Viscount 781D – originally delivered to No. 28 Squadron but later becoming the flagship of No. 21 Squadron – is, with its low number of flying hours, in superlative condition.

Overleaf: The penultimate official flight of the world's last three remaining airworthy Avro Shackleton MR Mk. 3s, from No. 35 Squadron, took place on 22 November 1984. Two of these much-loved aircraft are shown flying line astern on that occasion. An Impala Mk. 1 from No. 7 Squadron joins in, in loose formation. They were photographed from the lead Shackleton's tail cone – a flimsy-looking, badly scratched and cracked construction of perspex conducive neither to good visibility nor to sharp photography.

2

1   3

1 Disturbed air whips up spray to create a rainbow as this Alouette III from No. 87 Helicopter Flying School pirouettes in the bowl of the Sterkspruit Falls near Champagne Castle in the Drakensberg.

2 Seventeen Alouette IIIs from No. 17 Squadron in loose formation near the Magaliesberg, on their way to a ceremonial fly-past over their base at Swartkop, in 1983, to celebrate their 21st anniversary in SAAF service.

1 A Westland Wasp banks over the 'dolosse' – interlocking artificial breakwater stanchions – near the Court Helicopters' heli-pad at Cape Town's docks.

2 Largest and heaviest helicopter in South Africa at present is the three-engined Aerospatiale SA321L Super Frelon. It can lift 5 000 kg of internal- or external-slung freight, or accommodates 27 troops.

3 The Aerospatiale Puma has proved to be one of the SAAF's most versatile helicopters. Here one of the craft from No. 31 Squadron enters a very steep bank over the flat terrain near its base at Hoedspruit.

1 The Cessna 185 Skywagon was originally imported in 1962 to replace the Austers as Air Observation Post aircraft, and have soldiered on over the years to become trainers used by No. 84 Light Aircraft Training School at Potchefstroom. The Cessna 185 – the SAAF's most economical craft – has also done useful general communications work in the operational area.

2 The Atlas-designed and built C-4M Kudu is the SAAF's standard light battlefield transport aircraft. Affectionately known as 'the converter' (it converts Avgas into decibels), this eight-seater is the epitome of ruggedness and reliability, even though its box-like fuselage demands real pilot skill during cross-wind landings.

3 Replacing the Cessna 185 as the SAAF's Forward Air Control and Air Observation Post aircraft is the Italian Aeritalia/Aermacchi AM-3CM Bosbok. The South African Air Force is now the only operator of this type, after the sole other user, the Rwanda Air Force, withdrew the three it had. Here a Bosbok banks steeply over the typical bush terrain near Eenhana in Northern Namibia.

1, 2 and 3 Few people realise that much of the Allied effort's air success during the Second World War depended upon just one type of aircraft: the North American Harvard, used to train combat pilots, and train them exceptionally well. After more than four decades of faithful service the venerable Harvard still remains the SAAF's *ab initio* trainer and may well continue in that rôle for many years to come. This fully aerobatic craft has always been a firm favourite of South African air shows. Pictures show: Harvard 7688 from the Central Flying School at Dunnottar, flown by Major Ray Houghton.

Overleaf: A MiG 17 of the Moçambique People's Liberation Air Force, flown here by a South African test pilot, keeps company with a Mirage F-1AZ from No. 1 Squadron. Lieutenant Adriano Bomba's defection to South Africa in 1983 was initially detected by radar. Two of No. 1 Squadron's F-1AZs were scrambled to intercept the MiG, which was ordered to proceed to Hoedspruit. After evaluation by the SAAF's Test Flight and Development Centre, it was returned by road to Maputo.

5 FOR THE LOVE OF FLYING
Recreational aviation
Vintage, experimental and home-built

Left: SAA's CASA 352L, ZS-UYU (alias Ju52/3m, ZS-AFA) flies over the tranquil Hartebeespoort Dam.

Above: Problems with the Spanish-built ENMA *Beta* engines prompted the decision to refit, temporarily, the CASA 352L with the trusted Pratt & Whitney R-1340.

Overleaf: Arguably one of the most beautiful aircraft ever designed, a Spitfire Mk. 9 flies low over the Transvaal. Owned by Larry Barnett – who also had a hand in rebuilding the 'Spit' in the initial stages of the work – it is now on permanent loan to the SAAF. It is finished in the exact camouflage and markings of the aircraft flown during the Second World War by No. 40 Squadron commander Bob Rogers.

1 Once part of the East African Airways Corporation fleet, this de Havilland DH89A Dragon Rapide ended its airline career inter-island hopping in the Seychelles with Air Mahé. Vintage aircraft enthusiast John English acquired the Tanzanian-registered Rapide, 5H-AAN, in early 1975 and flew it to South Africa from the Seychelles. Today this Rapide, ZS-JGV, is the last airworthy machine of its type in Africa.

2 Immaculately restored to its original war-time finish and authentic British military serial number KK552, this Fairchild 24R Argus III is seen near Margate, Natal, where it took part in one of the Experimental Aircraft Association's annual fly-ins. Regrettably officialdom requires the prominent display of current civilian registrations on restored vintage aircraft.

3 Few aviation enthusiasts ever have the opportunity to see a genuine First World War fighter in flight these days. This has been remedied to a degree by 'Zingy' Harrison's immaculate and appropriately registered Sopwith Pup replica, ZS-PUP, seen here flying over the lush cane fields near its home base, Margate. The original First World War Pup was powered by an 80 hp Le Rhône, but the replica has a more modern 300 hp engine, and there is never any need to fly the aircraft at more than half throttle.

1 The de Havilland DH82A Tiger Moth was the SAAF's standard
ab initio training aircraft throughout the Second World War, and many of
them were sold to private owners after 1945. One such Tiger is ZS-DLC, now
based at a small airstrip near Grabouw in the Western Cape.

2 Student-instructor communications during flight in an open-cockpit
aircraft is a problem at the best of times, partly solved by the introduction
of the 'Gosport'-tube. This Tiger Moth pilot wears the typical period
garb of the barnstorming era.

3 Many owners like to portray their Tiger Moths' original ancestry, and
several of the old machines are now finished in semi-military colours.
To aid visibility, training aircraft were painted yellow. Here Bob Ewing
banks his Tiger, ZS-DNX, steeply over Hartebeespoort Dam.

4 Soon after the Second World War broke out, all civilian aircraft in
South Africa were impressed into the SAAF for military service. This
de Havilland DH87B Hornet Moth came to South Africa in 1937 as
ZS-ALA and survived the war period, to revert to civilian ownership
until the SAAF Museum acquired it in January 1981. It was restored to
its authentic war-time markings, seen here, in the Museum workshops
at Lanseria.

1 3

4

1 The Fieseler Fi-156c-7 Storch was one of the first airworthy aircraft of the SAAF Museum. One of the many Luftwaffe machines taken over by Britain after the Second World War, it came to South Africa in November 1946. The colour scheme is the standard one for Luftwaffe liaison aircraft flown on the Eastern Front.

2 Chipmunk WG354, photographed flying over Table Bay, was restored to its original finish – as a trainer with the RAF's Rhodesian Air Training Group – by No. 35 Squadron, SAAF, and is now part of the ever-growing fleet of airworthy SAAF Museum aircraft.

1
2

111

1

1 The Globe Swift flew for the first time in January 1945. Just over a thousand had been built, mostly by Temco Aircraft Corporation, when production ceased in 1951. Here a Swift GC-1B is seen over the rocks on the Natal South Coast.

2 This Beechcraft model D17S Staggerwing ZS-PWD was recently exported to the United States, and only one remains active in South Africa. Deriving its name from the negative stagger of its wings, this machine, originally ordered in 1939 for the United States Navy as a liaison and communications aircraft, does a high-speed run along the coast near Margate.

3 Perhaps the classic of all light planes, this Piper J-3C Cub, ZS-BJA, flies along the beach near the Wild Coast. The Cub is powered by a 65 hp Continental engine. The J-3 Cub design dates back to before the Second World War, appearing for the first time in 1938. By the time it was superseded by the more powerful PA-18 Super Cub, 19 798 civil and military Cubs had come off the production line.

1 The side-by-side cockpit seating arrangement has rendered the Vampire T Mk. 55 eminently suitable for the testing of avionics and, up to 1984, two of the machines were used by the Test Flight and Development Centre of the SAAF. The de Havilland Vampire was the SAAF's first operational jet and several, among them the two TFDC aircraft, are now with the SAAF Museum. Here the Vampire T Mk. 55, No. 257, displays the TFDC's colour scheme.

2 The Alouette II was the SAAF's first turbine-powered helicopter. A small number was delivered to No. 17 Squadron in 1961 to join the unit's three Sikorsky S-55Cs. With the arrival of the first Alouette IIIs soon afterwards, the Alouette IIs were used as helicopter trainers before being passed to the Rhodesian security forces in the early 1970s. They were returned when hostilities ceased, and this immaculately finished Alouette II is now flying with the SAAF Museum.

3 This ex-Fleet Air Arm Sikorsky S-55 Whirlwind HAS Mk. 22 has been restored to flying condition by No. 19 Squadron, and is painted to represent A5, one of the three S-55Cs flown by the SAAF in the late 1950s. This machine was originally imported from Britain by Autair Helicopters but never flew commercially in South Africa. When civil certification eventually became unfeasible, the helicopter, together with another, similar, model, was donated to the SAAF Museum. A5 is seen here flying over the SAAF Memorial on Bays Hill, Swartkop Air Force Base.

4 It is difficult to believe that this Harvard Mk. IIA, seen here in the late-1950s colours of No. 8 Squadron SAAF, is a British civil aircraft, registered G-BGOU. Owner Peter Snell decided to restore its authentic SAAF finish after acquiring it from the Portuguese Air Force (which had received a number of SAAF Harvards in the early 1970s). Snell was tragically killed when the machine crashed on 9 September 1985 near Bourn Airfield, during a practice aerobatic display while en route from RAF Finningley to Debden.

1 The KR-2 is an extremely popular amateur construction design: it is thought that there are more of them being built by non-professionals than any other model. Here Ray Houghton banks Sakkie Halgreen's KR-2 during a fly-past near Margate, with another KR-2 following.

2 One of the many remarkable, and unconventional, aircraft designed by Burt Rutan is the LongEze, a long-range version of his earlier, and very successful, VariEze design, both of which have been built by amateur constructors. Two LongEzes are here seen flying low over the South Coast beaches.

3 A top view of a Model 61 LongEze graphically illustrates this aircraft's unorthodox engine and canard layout.

4 This Luton Beta, ZS-UFG, was built by the Rautenbach brothers (seen here being flown by Clive) at Virginia Airport, Durban.

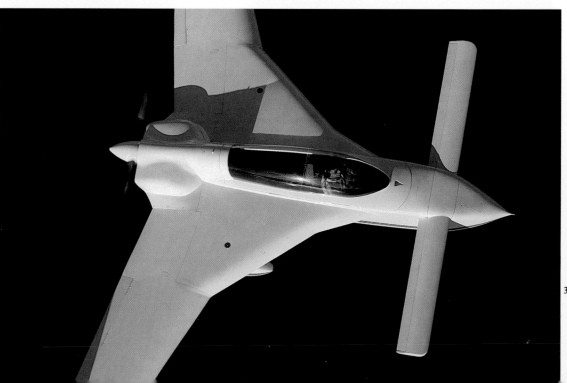

1 This Teenie Two, ZS-UHC, flown by Derek Hopkins, is probably the smallest aircraft on the South African civil aircraft register.

2 This Auster J/1 Autocrat was once with the Southern Rhodesian Air Force, which retired it in 1955. After some years as a Rhodesian civil aircraft, it came to South Africa in February 1974. The Autocrat was a post-war version of the wartime Auster Mk. 5. Bill Keil's immaculate machine has been modified with a more powerful Lycoming engine.

3, 4, 5, 6 and 7 A miscellany of designs constructed by amateur builders. The photographs show, in a numerical order: an EAA Biplane (ZS-UEX); Evans VP-1 (ZS-UIH); Bakeng Duce (ZS-UHK); Bowers Fly Baby 1A (ZS-UFI), and a Cassut Renergade (ZS-UGV).

Aerobatics

Left: Manfred Strössenreuther in a Zlin 50L in action at the South
African World Masters Aerobatic Tournament, held at La Mercy Airfield
near Durban.

Above: The 1985/86 South African aerobatic champion in the 'unlimited'
category is Peter Celliers, who owns one of the few Zlin 50Ls in the Western
world. Here he rolls the aircraft near La Mercy Airfield.

1 A Pitts Special flies upside-down above a Harvard.

2 Dennis Spence banking his Smirnoff Pitts over Hartebeespoort Dam.

3 André van Kraayenburg rolls his Pitts S1-A while practising for the South African World Masters Aerobatic Tournament.

1 The Winfield Magnum aerobatic team is fast becoming one of the most popular attractions at air shows and promotion events. The team comprises leader Scully Levin, Chris Rademan and Jeff Birch. Here they demonstrate a beautiful 'switchblade'.

2 Winfield Magnum performing a 'waterfall break' and . . .

3 . . . a formation barrel roll.

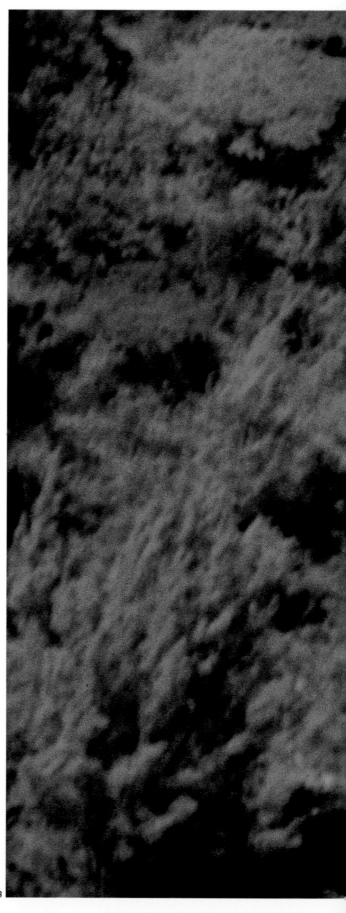

1 Nick Turvey in the brightly-coloured Pitts he flew before crashing it during the 1981 Lanseria Air Show. Nick survived the accident – which destroyed the aircraft – and has recovered fully.

2 A glaze-eyed Herman Potgieter after a lengthy spell of upside-down aviating over Hartebeestpoort Dam in Scully Levin's Pitts Special. Levin is renowned for, among other feats, his ability to land his Piper J-3C Cub on the back of a moving truck (see page 12).

3 André Bekker, one of about 35 active aerobatic pilots in South Africa, pulls up for a stall turn in a Pitts S1-B near Ballitoville on the Natal coast.

Gliding

Left: One of the great thrills of gliding is the chandelle, or wing-over. Donaldson Dam and the Randfontein-Vereeniging highway are clearly visible in the background.

Above: Karl-Heinz Hirsch, ex-Luftwaffe Me 262 jet fighter pilot, lands his glider at the Sun City Cascades Hotel golf course.

Overleaf: Slowly and gracefully two Grob motorized gliders pass over a river near Margate, Natal.

1 Some of the exhilarating freedom of powerless flight is conveyed by this upside-down Grob Astir performing a loop near Donaldson Dam.

2 A Fournier accurately cuts tape with its wing during the Sun City Air Show.

3 For those on the ground the sun has already set, but the two enthusiasts in this Grob Twin Astir still have to shield their eyes when looking up at the photo-glider.

4 Viewed head-on, and waiting for a tug hook-up at Donaldson Dam airstrip. Today's typical high-performance glider has a moulded glass-fibre shell, is sleekly aerodynamic, has a stalling speed of around 60 km/h and a maximum safe speed of 250 km/h.

5 A cloud-topping Fournier motor glider. Diversity of terrain and meteorological conditions make South Africa something of a mecca for overseas gliding enthusiasts, and many world records have been set in the country's skies.

Microlights

Above: Microlight flying is a thrilling sport but not a dangerous one: the sensation, in one pilot's words, is 'like riding a bicycle 300 metres above the ground'. In the six years up to 1985 only six people were killed in accidents, most during the sport's infancy, when pilots were largely self-taught.

Opposite page: The MFS Shadow is locally designed and built. Here pilot Ian Drennan puts it through its paces above the Natal coast.

Overleaf: A stall-turn in a Quicksilver MX II is for many the ultimate microlighting experience, especially for a passenger who is up on her first flight.

1 John Pocock flies a Quicksilver MX II near Mooi River. Microlighting and hang gliding share a common origin, parting company in the early 1970s with the development of ultra-light materials and better wing designs. By 1979 the machines had belt-driven reduction drives, strong undercarriages, efficient wing sections and hand-throttles.

2 Keeping warm in a microlight is essential. The chill created by moving at speed through very cold air can cause drowsiness, and slow the reactions. Pictured is a Quicksilver MX II.

1 2

1 A Dragon 150 – showing more than a hint of the First World War in its design – cruises over Midmar Dam. Says one enthusiast: 'Microlighters have a common love and camaraderie, the pride and warmth of belonging to a group who came has as close to natural flight as possible.'

2 Locally designed and built, this MAC CDL flies over harvested wheat-fields near Durbanville, Cape. South Africa's microlight manufacturing industry is small but dynamic; exchange rates favour *in situ* production – for both local sales and export.

3 A Quicksilver MX II flies past Howick Falls in Natal.

1 The Cosmos Trike is one of the more manoeuvrable microlights, and has become very popular in South Africa: it is relatively inexpensive, easy to maintain and to fly.

2 Also highly regarded by enthusiasts is the Beaver.

3 The Sirocco is marketed by Aviation 2000 and, says one owner, is 'at least a *real* little aeroplane'.

4 One of the most acclaimed of South African designs is the Thunderbird, produced by Louis Meyer of Sport Aviation SA. The Thunderbird could be the first to rival the entry-level training capabilities of the Cessna 152 and Piper 140.

5 With its transparent wings and canard design, the Falcon is one of the most attractive of the new-generation microlights.

6 Also among the more pleasing and efficient of the machines is the Pioneer Flightstar, shown approaching a stall-turn with Tim James at the stick.

Hang gliding

Left: Western Province champion Dale Lippstreu hang glides over the Cedarberg on a journey from Porterville to Clanwilliam, a distance of some 200 kilometres.

Above: A hang glider comes in to land at Sea Point, Cape Town.

1 A panoramic view of Dasklip Pass near Porterville, which has superb visibility and strong thermals, and is arguably the best hang gliding area in South Africa.

2 All the excitement of hang gliding is conveyed by this picture of John Williamson soaring over Sea Point and Green Point, Cape Town.

3 An original South African design, this hang glider performs a series of tight turns over Sea Point.

4 Dasklip provides a fine take-off slope. South African pilots took part in world championships in 1976, 1983 and 1985, and are rated internationally among the top ten.

1

147

Ballooning

Above: Ballooning involves early starts – with the grass still wet from the dew, the sun golden and warming, and the gas burners roaring, ready to inflate the nylon fabric. This photograph was taken in the Waterberg, northern Transvaal.

Opposite page: Balloons rise above Sun City.

Overleaf: Over a thousand square metres of colourful nylon fabric fills up with heated air. The first locally-made balloon made its maiden flight in 1977.

1 Bill Harrop opens the taps prior to taking off with a full load of passengers on one of his renowned balloon-safari flights. His was the first non-scheduled balloon 'airline' in South Africa.

2 Skimming the Sun City lake during late afternoon. 'Champagne flights' are popular and, for the owners, profitable.

3 Three balloonists in close proximity start a provincial championship flight. The first national championships were held in 1977, drawing just four entrants. Currently they attract around twenty balloonists, from whom a team is chosen to represent South Africa at the world championships.

4 Balloons can be used for the test purposes, and to lift hang gliders in areas where there is no high ground.

1 Tony Corrie became a South African citizen the day before setting a new altitude record of 21 600 feet (6 583 metres) in this Procolor balloon.

2 As in other countries, South African balloons are often sponsored, carrying their sponsor's colours. Here the Johannesburg Centenary balloon shares airspace near Orient, Transvaal, during a provincial championship.

3 Tony Corrie about to undertake a stand-up landing after breaking the South African balloon altitude record.

Skydiving

1 Spectacular scenery and skydiving often go together. Here a reconnaissance team jump from a SAAF Dakota over Saldanha Bay.

2 A stick of twenty skydivers leaps off the rear ramp of a Safair L100-30 Hercules. Because of the aircraft's relatively high speed while on jump-run, it is essential for the divers to exit as close to each other as possible in order to minimise spread after jumping. Even after an efficient exit, the first and last jumper out can be separated, horizontally, by as much as fifty metres.

3 Tumbling bodies show the extreme turbulence encountered after a mass exit from the rear of a Safair L100-30 Hercules. The apparent chaos soon resolves into a dynamic free-fall formation: each skydiver 'flying' relative to the others and filling a specific part of the sequence in order to complete a pre-planned pattern in the sky.

157

1 A student skydiver launches out on his first jump, from a Cessna 182, near Pietermaritzburg. The static-line, which is attached to the aircraft and which deploys the parachute automatically, can clearly be seen. The spread-arched position is a vital aspect of skydiving – it ensures stability, especially when the student progresses to free-fall.

2 A two-man 'stack' lands at Sun City. This latest development of the sport is known as canopy relative work, or CRW. It is a spontaneous off-shoot of skydiving and evolved as a direct result of the introduction of the Ram-air canopy or 'square' parachute. The South African record for the biggest canopy stack currently (1986) stands at eleven.

INDEX

159

The South African designed and produced Alpha-XH1 helicopter. The aircraft was first shown to the public in March 1986 (too late to be included in the body of this book), and is the culmination of a decade-long experimental and development effort.

In fact the process could be said to have had its beginnings in the early 1960s, when there were several attempts to produce South African-designed rotorcraft. The Rotorcraft Minicopter was a small single-seat gyrocopter powered by a 72 hp engine, and several appeared on the South African civil aircraft register after the prototype's maiden flight in September 1962. Shortly afterwards the Helicopter Manufacturing Company designed and manufactured a two-seat light utility helicopter powered by a 150 hp Lycoming piston engine. Known as the Vos Springbok, flight trials began early in 1964, but the project was abandoned due to lack of sponsorship after only one prototype was flown. Timely realisation that politics might jeopardize the procurement of aircraft for the SAAF led to the establishment of the Atlas Aircraft Corporation in 1965 with its prime initial object to produce, under licence from Aermacchi in Italy, the MB326M Impala Mk. 1 jet trainer for the SAAF. This was superseded by the light attack derivative, the MB326KC Impala Mk. 2, produced alongside the South African-designed C4M Kudu light battlefield communications aircraft.

Meanwhile, the Council for Scientific and Industrial Research was designing several one-off research autogyros, the first appearing on the civil register early in 1972. Three different autogyros were built by the time the project was completed, and it may be speculated that much of the research gained was aimed at establishing South Africa's own helicopter industry.

The first real breakthrough in the continued quest to overcome the United Nations arms embargo against South Africa came when, in total secrecy, a locally designed and developed light attack helicopter, the Atlas Alpha-XH1, took to the air for the first time.

The Alpha-XH1 is a tandem two-seat helicopter and in common with other attack helicopters (such as the Hughes AH-64, Agusta A 129 and IAR 317 Airfox) is flown from the rear with a weapon system operator seated in front, although dual controls allow it to be flown from either position.

The prototype Alpha-XH1 shown here is armed with a single GA-1 servo-controlled cannon mounted under the forward fuselage and has an impressive field of movement – an elevation of $+10°$ to $-60°$ and a sweep arc of $120°$ each side of the centre line. The South African-developed GA-1, which is an improved version of the well known and proven MG 151 automatic cannon, is capable of a 700 round-per-minute rate of fire and is linked to the unique locally-designed helmet sight which enables the gunner to direct the cannon onto the target by merely looking at it. The cannon is noted for its compactness and, above all, low recoil forces. Despite a low muzzle velocity of 720 metres per second, the armour piercing shells are capable of considerable penetration. General specifications for the helicopter (except the maximum take-off weight, which is 2 200 kg) and performance figures had not at the time of going to press been released by the manufacturer. The Alpha-XH1 has roughly the size and performance of the Alouette III and, superficially, it appears that some features, such as the power plant, tail boom, main and tail rotors, rotor head and main undercarriage are derived from the Alouette III. However, during the public unveiling of the Alpha-XH1 on 8 March 1986, the Chief of the South African Air Force, Lt. Gen. Denis Earp, emphasised that the design, development and manufacture of the helicopter is totally South African.

The Alpha-XH1 is only a development prototype and will not necessarily enter production in its present configuration. The initial contract for the design and manufacture of the Alpha-XH1 was signed in March 1981, and since its first flight on the 3 February 1985 has completed initial flight testing. This test and evaluation programme continues and it is likely that other weapons systems, such as anti-tank missiles, carried on stub wings, will be added before a final production model emerges.